Evaluating Teachers of Writing

Evaluating Teachers of Writing

Edited by

Christine A. Hult
Utah State University

National Council of Teachers of English
1111 W. Kenyon Road, Urbana, Illinois 61801-1096

Editorial and Typesetting Services: Robert A. Heister
Humanities & Sciences Associates

NCTE Production Editors: Michael G. Ryan, Michelle Sanden Johlas

Interior Design: Tom Kovacs for TGK Design

Cover Design: Jim Proefrock

NCTE Stock Number: 16213–3050

Library of Congress Cataloging-in-Publication Data

Evaluating teachers of writing / edited by Christine Hult.
    p.   cm.
    Includes bibliographical references and index.
    "NCTE stock number 16213-3050—T. p. verso.
    ISBN 0–8141–1621–3
    1. English language—Rhetoric—Study and teaching—United States—
Evaluation. 2. English teachers —United States—Rating of. 3. College teachers—United States—Rating of.   I. Hult, Christine A.
PE1405.U6E93   1994
808'.042'07—dc20

                                                           93–27235
                                                              CIP

Contents

I Background and Theory

1 Introduction

Christine A. Hult
Utah State University

Evaluating teachers is a problematic and often controversial enterprise. The motivations for evaluation range from punitive to constructive, and emotions often run high because the stakes can be enormous: employment decisions, remediation, faculty retention, improvement of teaching and learning, accountability, fairness, and competition are all issues that come into play when discussing evaluation of teachers.

The emotional charge of this issue exploded recently on my own campus, when a group of student leaders from the student senate took it upon themselves to write letters to the top and bottom thirty teachers as rated by the numerical ranking on the universitywide student-evaluation-of-teachers form. This action caused a flurry of discussion among faculty and student groups and between the administration and students, with the positive result that many groups are taking a closer look at considerations of what it means to "evaluate" teachers. Who should do the evaluating? What form or forms should that evaluation take? Or, should there be any evaluation at all of teachers by students or anyone else? How is evaluation itself related to improving teaching? To improving learning? In an attempt to answer these questions, the present collection provides teachers, administrators, and students with some ways of thinking through the problems and issues facing higher education, generally, and the discipline of teaching writing, specifically, as we seek to devise equitable and useful evaluation procedures.

Although the issue of teacher evaluation is troublesome, even more so, for a number of reasons, is the issue of evaluating teachers of writing. First, there are political and ideological reasons that make evaluating writing teachers a problem. The instructors who teach writing on college and university campuses are all too often marginalized groups: part-time lecturers or adjunct faculty hired for pitiful wages under deplorable working conditions or graduate teaching assistants exploited as cheap labor while they work on their advanced degrees.

Second, there are pedagogical reasons that make evaluation of writing teachers problematic. The composition profession has not arrived at a uniform consensus about teaching methodology in writing; rather, there are a number of competing, equally viable models, ranging from student centered to teacher-directed. One evaluation procedure or set of criteria will not serve for all teachers any more than it will serve for all pedagogies. For example, when an administrator is observing a writing teacher conducting a peer workshop, an evaluation questionnaire that asks if "the instructor exhibits mastery of content" is virtually meaningless. How can a writing teacher exhibit mastery of content in a single class session? The questions need to be changed to fit the particular writing class being observed.

Finally, there are questions about evaluators' motives that confuse the issue of evaluating teachers of writing. What are our reasons for evaluating, anyway? What do we hope to accomplish? There are two related but conflicting goals that underlie teacher evaluation: one is the goal of accountability, achieved through summative evaluations of performance; the other is the goal of improvement in classroom teaching and learning, achieved through formative evaluations of performance.

According to the *American Educators' Encyclopedia* (Dejnozka and Kapel 1991), the terms *formative* and *summative evaluation* were introduced by Michael Scriven in a 1967 AERA monograph. The *Encyclopedia* defines formative evaluation as "assessment that takes place during the developmental (formative) stages of a program or a product" (226). Information gathered during a formative assessment "may then be used to alter a program, to revise materials, to restructure a program design, or to reconsider goals and objectives" (226).

In contrast, summative evaluation is defined as "the assessment of the overall effectiveness of a program or a product. Unlike formative evaluation, which is carried out during the development of a program, summative evaluation takes place after a program is fully developed and implemented" (551–52). The *Encyclopedia* points out that "the results of summative evaluations usually are a major concern for policymakers, and the results of formative evaluations are of particular interest to . . . those working in the program" (552).

As I am using these terms, formative evaluation of writing teachers occurs as they are teaching and is designed to provide information that may help them to alter their teaching in ways that improve student learning. Summative evaluation of writing teachers occurs as a one-time assessment to judge overall teaching performance with the purpose of "summing up" the effectiveness of that performance, usually as a way to guide administrators in personnel decisions. Most assessment instruments, and the resultant data, can be used for either formative or summative evaluation purposes.

Too often in teacher evaluation, because the formative is not separated from the summative, the two goals of accountability and improvement are conflated when they may not necessarily be compatible. For example, a summative performance review of a teacher who has received numerous complaints may have as its purpose the documenting of the teacher's inadequacies for purposes of terminating his or her employment. We should not delude ourselves into thinking that such an evaluation is meant to help the teacher improve. On the other hand, a formative evaluation of teaching is intended to provide the teacher with valuable feedback that the teacher can use in self-improvement efforts. In formative evaluations, one gets another chance, an opportunity to "revise" one's performance. And a serious effort at formative evaluation can mediate the necessity for summative evaluation, because the evaluator is able to see the shaping of a teacher over time, in a rich and varied context.

Peter Elbow (1986) encourages us to "embrace contraries" in the teaching of writing. One of the main contraries that he identifies is that of being at the same time both a coach and a judge to our students. We face a similar contrary when we are placed in the role of teacher-evaluator. What Elbow advocates is an up-front admission of the two conflicting roles when teaching writing: We adopt our coach role as the students are prewriting, composing, drafting, revising; then, when the entire process is completed—as far as the student is able, given constraints, deadlines, and desires—the teacher's role must switch from coach to judge. Ultimately, the teacher needs to evaluate the product produced by the entire process.

In teacher evaluation, as in teaching writing, we need to be aware of the contraries. We genuinely want our teachers to improve, just as we want our student writers to improve. But on occasion, we may need to adopt the role of judge and make a difficult evaluative decision to replace an ineffective or inept teacher. Taking a lesson from Elbow and the writing process, when beginning any evaluation system, it seems to me that we first need to separate the coach from the judge, the formative evaluation from the summative, if our goal genuinely is improvement in instruction. Again, as with teaching writing, there is eventual accountability: the coach at some point becomes the judge.

But if we only undertake summative evaluations—as is all too often the case in writing programs that use only student evaluations and perhaps an occasional classroom visit without providing teachers opportunities to receive focused feedback from a peer-pair, to team teach, to practice new teaching techniques in their classes, or to demonstrate improvement—we are committing the same error that process writing pedagogy seeks to correct. To my mind, performing only summative evaluation is analogous to the writing teacher who evaluates only finished products, writes copious commentary, and perhaps even conferences with the student on the paper, hoping that somehow the writer's next paper will improve. But as we have learned, product evaluation has little or no effect on writing improvement unless the student is allowed to rewrite. What does help is commentary, conferencing—feedback— during the process of writing and rewriting the paper. Similarly, in my own role as the director of a writing program, I am beginning to recognize that my frustration with evaluating teachers has come from my inability to separate the summative evaluation (product) from the formative evaluation (process). Collecting student evaluations, observing teachers in their classrooms, perhaps even conferencing with teachers on student evaluations and peer observations, seemed to have little effect on teacher improvement, perhaps because I was not using these evaluation methods formatively. Rather, I was using them as a summation of teacher performance, just as one would sum up the reasons for a student's grade on a paper, but not as a way to provide feedback that the teacher could use to improve.

As I reread Weimer's (1990) book, I was struck by how the mythology Weimer applies to teaching resembles the mythology applied to writing, a mythology that may be contributing to our confusion of purposes as we evaluate teachers of writing:

> *Myths about Teaching and Writing*
> Myth 1: Teaching is a gift; Good teachers are born, not made.
>   (Writing is a gift; Good writers are born, not made.)
> Myth 2: If you know about it, you can teach it.
>   (If you know about it, you can write about it.)
> Myth 3: Faculty teach subjects, not students.
>   (Writers write forms, not ideas.) (Weimer 1990, 4–7;
>   the parenthetical items are mine.)

Certainly we can all cite examples of gifted teachers, and gifted writers, but contrary to the mythology about teaching and writing, learning to teach, like learning to write, is a developmental skill that everyone can improve on to some degree. Similarly, being well-versed in a subject does not automatically mean that you can communicate your knowledge to others, especially if you espouse the position that your job is to teach your subject, not your students. Again, we can learn a lot about teaching by reflecting on what we know about writing: communication comes through a rhetorical process balancing the needs of the audience with the intentions of the writer (or the needs of the students with the intentions of the teacher).

Weimer emphasizes that if improvement is the desired outcome, teachers must voluntarily participate in the process. We know this with our students: we can make suggestions for revisions, but unless they truly want to improve a piece of writing, nothing we say will matter. All faculty should be invited to participate, but each instructor should be put in charge of his or her own instructional improvement plan. Individuals should decide the extent of the changes and the means employed to accomplish those changes. The coach-improver should serve as a resource person, just as the writing coach serves as a resource person, making suggestions for change but ultimately allowing the student, or in this case the teacher, ownership of his or her own improvement process. When we are working closely with teachers in a coach-improver role, we see them creating a "text" of their own teaching, just as we see writers create a text as we coach them through subsequent drafts.

A teacher's "text" can be captured in the form of a teaching portfolio. In a recent publication, Edgerton, Hutchings, and Quinlan (1991) describe how teachers can develop a written record of their teaching through assembling such a portfolio. Just as the teacher evaluation process parallels in many ways the evaluation of writing, so, too, the teaching portfolio can be seen as parallel to the writing portfolio. Portfolios of both types seek to capture the complexity of teaching and writing and, furthermore, to encourage the portfolio's compiler to self-reflect on the meaning of its contents. Edgerton, Hutchings, and Quinlan call this "reflective practice," the necessary precursor of improvement.

Weimer outlines five steps to instructional improvement, and, once again, we see that each step parallels steps often seen in the writing process:

Steps for Instructional Improvement
1. Developing instructional awareness [through self-reflection]. (Developing metacognitive strategies and awareness of your own writing processes.)
2. Gathering information [from colleagues and students]. (Gathering information through the invention and discovery stages of writing.)

3. Making choices about changes.
   (Deciding what to change and how, through revision plans.)

4 Implementing the alterations [in the classroom].
   (Incorporating changes into writing.)

5. Assessing the alterations [through assessment of peer and
   student feedback].
   (Determining through self-assessment of writing and
   through peer evaluations and feedback what impact
   changes will have on the text.) (Weimer 1990, 34–41; brack-
   eted and parenthetical items are mine.)

Following are some of the advantages to be gained by instituting a
formative evaluation process (adapted from Weimer, 22–27).

Better teaching is seen as something to which everyone can aspire. New
teachers should not feel singled out; every teacher can improve, just as
every writer can improve, regardless of the current level of skill. One
success story on my campus involved an experienced teacher who
observed the peer-workshop class of a colleague. The experienced teacher
realized after only ten minutes of visitation that she needed to drastically
rethink how she was conducting her own peer-workshop classes in light
of the highly successful methods she observed.

Support is offered for any and all faculty efforts at improvement. Sharing of
ideas among teachers becomes acceptable. Teaching is a community
activity, just as in workshop classes where writing is a community
activity; teaching should not be viewed as an individual activity with
each teacher isolated in a private classroom, just as writing should not be
seen as an exclusively private act with an individual writer isolated in a
garret. In a writing workshop, writers share ideas about their writing; in
a department that operates as an ongoing "teaching workshop," teachers
should also share information about their teaching. There is much talk in
the profession about collaborative writing; there should also be talk
about collaborative teaching.

Teachers are in charge of their own improvement process. Teachers must be
encouraged to reflect on what they are doing and should be given com-
pensatory time to do so. When others are trying to improve, there is subtle
peer pressure for all teachers to improve. In this model, the performance
evaluator becomes a resource person, a coach rather than a judge.

We can learn from our own teaching of writing when we initiate the
evaluation process for teachers. Let's embrace the contraries and not
ignore them. Let's not try to fool ourselves into thinking that our
summative evaluations will somehow improve teaching; they won't,

any more than our summative evaluations (extensive comments on final drafts) will improve our students' writing. What is the motivation to revise once a completed paper has been turned in or a completed evaluation letter written?

This is not to deny the necessary role of the judge. There are times when summative evaluation is essential for continuing employment decisions. It may also be useful, for example, to have a letter from an administrator in each teacher's personnel file, attesting to his or her teaching abilities. However, this summative evaluation process should not be expected to improve instruction very much. To improve instructional effectiveness, we have to separate the coach from the judge, acknowledging both roles and the importance of each, but recognizing their differences and how they should be employed to best advantage in the improvement process.

To address the complexity of the issues surrounding evaluating teachers of writing, I have divided this book into three parts. Part I includes background and theory germane to teacher evaluation. David Bleich, explores the underlying ideologies, hidden and overt, that precipitate an atmosphere of evaluation. Jesse Jones, speaking from the perspective of a seasoned administrator, argues for the purposes and goals of such evaluation.

Part II treats various evaluation methods, from peer reviews (Ellen Strenski, Anne Marie Flanagan, Michael Vivion) to student evaluations (Edward White, Peter Elbow), to videotaped microteaching (Mark Baker and Joyce Kinkead). It seems clear from these chapters that we need first to take a careful look at our evaluation goals and match goals with methods. The authors advocate multiple measures of teaching performance, not single measures, to give a more complete picture of a teacher's effectiveness and/or to help that teacher improve.

Part III investigates some of the diverse faculty groups that tend to make up teaching staff in writing programs. David Schwalm suggests ways in which the needs of adjunct faculty can be accounted for in teaching evaluation; Irwin Weiser describes how teaching assistants can be brought into the teacher improvement process; John Bean explores the challenges faced when evaluating teachers in writing-across-the-curriculum programs; and Deborah Holdstein discusses the special issues involved in evaluating teachers who teach in computerized, networked writing classrooms.

In this book, I hope to make clear that there is no one right way to evaluate teachers of writing. It is an enormously complex task with competing purposes, goals, and methods. In the introduction to their book *Evaluating Writing,* Cooper and Odell (1977) affirm that "since writing is an expressive human activity, we believe the best response to it is a receptive, sympathetic, human response" (xii). Following the analogy of evaluating writing and evaluating teaching, this book also advocates the view that teaching is an expressive human activity that is equally deserving of a receptive, sympathetic, human response.

Works Cited

Cooper, Charles R., and Lee Odell, eds. 1977. *Evaluating Writing: Describing, Measuring, Judging.* Urbana: National Council of Teachers of English.

Dejnozka, Edward L., and David E. Kapel. 1991. *American Educators' Encyclopedia.* Rev. ed. New York: Greenwood Press.

Edgerton, Russell, Patricia Hutchings, and Kathleen Quinlan. 1991. *The Teaching Portfolio: Capturing the Scholarship in Teaching.* Washington, D.C.: American Association for Higher Education.

Elbow, Peter. 1986. *Embracing Contraries: Explorations in Learning and Teaching.* New York: Oxford University Press.

Scriven, Michael. 1967. "The Methodology of Evaluation." In *Perspectives of Curriculum Evaluation. AERA Monograph Series on Curriculum Evaluation, no. 1.* Chicago: Rand-McNally.

Weimer, Maryellen. 1990. *Improving College Teaching: Strategies for Developing Instructional Effectiveness.* San Francisco: Jossey-Bass.

2 Evaluating the Teaching of Writing: Questions of Ideology

David Bleich
University of Rochester

Many people concerned with the welfare of higher education have begun to reconsider postsecondary teaching. In spite of the appropriateness of this review, it is too often predicated on an alleged need to evaluate or assess teaching for the purpose of "improving" it. Instead of approaching this subject as one approaches other matters about which there is inadequate knowledge—in an interrogative or investigative spirit—the preferred approach to teaching by scholars and administrative higher-ups assumes that it needs evaluation and remediation. In fact, such alleged needs are the motive for reconsideration in the first place. For teachers of writing, as I will discuss shortly, this is even more intensely the case, but let me first consider how academic ideology circumscribes the wider issue of the assessment and remediation of teaching. I will then discuss how differently teaching writing might be conceived pursuant to a friendlier ideology—friendlier to all as well as one more responsive to feminist thought.

One of the more encouraging documents to participate in the current national review of university teaching is the "special report" by Ernest L. Boyer (1990) for the Carnegie Foundation for the Advancement of Teaching, entitled *Scholarship Reconsidered: Priorities of the Professoriate*. The report is based on a survey of faculty in five different classes of higher educational institutions, ranging from two-year colleges to research universities. The burden of the report is to recommend a more serious and elaborate attention to teaching in postsecondary education, even as it continues to reaffirm the priority of research and scholarship. While I welcome many of the recommendations in the report, it will pay us to dwell for a few moments on some of its language and presuppositions, which themselves help to create the problems they are trying to solve.

Boyer's report is based on a wide-ranging statistical study of faculty members in five types of postsecondary schools, ranked in terms of the degree of emphasis placed on research by the institution. Within each category there are two subcategories, a higher and a lower one, grouped according to different criteria (129–30). So there are actually nine categories of postsecondary schools in a hierarchical arrangement. The two categories of research universities are differentiated by how much federal support each receives for research. The "Doctorate-Granting Universities" are distinguished by how many degrees they grant in how many disciplines. "Comprehensive Universities and Colleges" (graduate level is master's degree only) are distinguished mainly by different sizes of enrollments; "Liberal Arts Colleges" (bachelor's degree only), also by enrollment sizes. The lowest category is "Two-Year Community, Junior, and Technical Colleges." The report does not emphasize directly the status difference in each rank and category, but it is hard to read the report without stipulating its presupposing such differences. While tables give the figures for each category (but not for the subcategories), the statistics are also often cited on an "average" basis: what faculty in all postsecondary school categories believe. There was, in my view, a responsible interpretation of the given data. The categories themselves, furthermore, seem sensible insofar as they describe accurately what kind of postsecondary schools exist in the United States, even insofar as the status of these categories is accepted by the public.

Here, then, is an immediate consideration: the report utilizes categories whose conditions of rank and status themselves make it seem that teaching is in need of remediation, a need the report is trying to answer. The report's call for a better reward system for teaching begins by urging the conceptualization of teaching as a form of scholarship; but more than to the need to change the category system, it is addressed to the morality of self-identification in universities. Though the deliberate search for status is rejected, the recommendations to give a higher priority to teaching bring neither the categories nor their status hierarchy under review.

> It's time to end the suffocating practice in which colleges and universities measure themselves far too frequently by external status rather than by values determined by their own distinctive mission. . . . But let's also candidly acknowledge that the degree to which this push for better education is achieved will be determined, in large measure, by the way scholarship is defined and, ultimately, rewarded. (Boyer 1990, xiii)

By redefining teaching as one of four kinds of scholarship, the "original" (highest) importances of research and scholarship are retained, while the sense of teaching as scholarship is meant to "raise" the status of teaching and to reflect this change by suitable professional rewards. But will "raising" the status of teaching have an effect on the category system presupposed by this report? It *can* have such an effect if it is accompanied by a noncompetitive means of identity formation in postsecondary school administrations and communities, an abandonment of the "self-measurement by external status." However, the report's higher ranking of research universities, for example, rather than comprehensive universities, suggests a permanent status scale that will urge and encourage competitive upward mobility. In order to end the measurement by external status, we need to learn to consider universities as having different functions from one another without different status.

But why might it be that Boyer and others who have addressed the matter of teaching in a constructive spirit nevertheless remain tacitly tied to the language and assumptions of competitive individualism? Competition is part of an ideology of social relations that is being challenged, for the first time in history on a broad scale, by those whom this ideology has not served—the representatives of disenfranchised constituencies. Here is Helen Longino's description of the ideology of competition in her 1987 essay of the same title:

> Social Darwinism provided the bourgeois classes with the legitimating social theory they needed. In feudal society hierarchical structure had been justified by concepts of nobility—one's birth determined one's station in life, and in particular one's position in the distribution and structure of power in society. In the modern world, the rising middle class needed a new system of legitimation that acknowledged their economic power and integrated it with the rightful exercise of political power. Names and offices were changed but the fundamentally pyramidal structure of society was not. Control of resources is still in the hands of the few—but now the notion of merit rather than birthright is used to legitimate membership in the ruling elites. And merit is, of course, determined by competition. How else?
>
> This, I think, is the ideology of competition—*ideology*, because it's not really descriptive of how power and control and access to resources are distributed and because our belief that it is descriptive does function to legitimize inequalities of distribution. (253)

Here Longino suggests that competition is *given as* the existing fair way to distribute wealth and privilege, but that it is only a piece of ideology because that is not, finally, how wealth and privilege are distributed. Because competition is attached to the fundamental economic welfare of Western society, it retains credibility when it is removed from its alleged economic basis and gets applied to other kinds of achievement. Thus, as Longino discusses, fellowships and tenure are *competitive*. "How else" does one distribute these "goods"? Similarly, Boyer and others, who in a good spirit want to "improve" teaching by using more formal evaluation, more judging, more prizes, are emulating the existing styles of "rewarding" research (thus suggesting more competition), are still working under the problematical assumptions of hierarchy and competition.

In Longino's description of Western society's change from feudal to bourgeois, she makes a point of the fact that there was no real change in the overall structure of society: it is still pyramidal. Competition entered as an approved feature because a new ideology was needed to retain the same social structure, but with the added *illusory* assurance that it is more accessible to more people. Competition, along with its ceremonies and structures, makes it seem that increased accessibility exists. But as is equally clear, competition is finally only a distraction from the obvious fact that only a few "win" contracts; only a few learn and study in research universities; only a few actually earn a living playing basketball; and only a few live without anxiety about earning a living, even in a privileged society like our own. Longino says: "In contemporary jargon, the ideology of competition functions as a mystification" (253).

According to some, competition enjoys an independent subjective and intersubjective life. People are sometimes considered "intrinsically" competitive. Walter Ong (1981) has gone as far as to say that *men* are *biologically* made for competition. Others cite women's competition for men as well as women's ability to participate in competitive sports as evidence for the universal and subjectively intrinsic status of competition. However, these arguments retain their force only if your political allegiance is to maintain the pyramidal structure of society as it has existed since civilization began. If, on the other hand, you consider yourself one of the unprivileged, and you are told that you must *compete* in order to achieve privilege, you may not believe that competition is anything more than one choice of behavioral style, appropriate and enjoyable in some venues but not in the main venues of public welfare and social justice.

In schools and universities, competition is the way certification and privilege are distributed. Here is how Longino describes it for faculty members:

> If we get tenure at our university teaching job, it's because we are the
> best qualified. If we don't get it, we just weren't good enough. The

> fact that our educational system is producing many more highly
> qualified scholars than it has room to employ or that U.S. institutions
> have a history of discriminating in favor of white middle-class males
> is generally ineffective in combating the sense of personal failure
> that losing in such a contest can bring about. (253)

Just as losing in job competition produces an unfair sense of defeat for
faculty members, low grades produce the same feeling for students,
whether they just did not win a contest or whether they did not get the
highest grades. In fact, in universities, many get, and should get, tenure
even though there was no determination as to the "best qualified."
Students with less than the highest grades succeed very well, as do many
students with downright low grades. As Longino observes, competition
does not actually determine what finally happens; it is merely the
*announced path of how distribution of privilege is supposed to take place, while
establishing a means of control from above.* Because of this announcement
and its ideological status to protect the academic pyramid, it is extremely
difficult to either adjust the actual process of privilege distribution or
make the announcements correspond more accurately with what actually happens. The ideology of competition burdens even the most well-
meaning initiatives for change.

Boyer's proposals are one of these initiatives, but his report's language
of the "pursuit of excellence," however generously intended, works
against such changes. This language participates in the ideology of
competition, and renders the need to assess, measure, and reward a
principal feature of all forms of scholarship as well as the "new" approach to teaching: "For teaching to be considered equal to research, it
must be vigorously assessed, using criteria that we recognize within the
academy, not just in a single institution" (Boyer 1990, 37). Even though
the report offers important suggestions for broadening the criteria of
evaluation in all forms of research and scholarship, it nevertheless
retains the sense that no matter how the university functions, the work
of its faculty must be subject to some kind of formal "external" evaluation. In the case of teaching, this approach is elaborated upon through a
discussion of "self-assessment, peer assessment, and student assessment," all reasonable and not necessarily competitive possible components of a collective attention to teaching.

Nevertheless, the values associated with increased attention to teaching are competitive. Here is one citation by Boyer:

> A president at a doctorate university, in commenting on the mission
> of his institution, put it this way: "This campus should be a place

> where both great teachers *and* great researchers function side by
> side." (58)

Boyer is emphasizing this president's wish for equality of teaching and
research. But the presupposed value embedded in the adjective "great"
is one of the fantasy values on which American society turns. This use of
"great" is not very different from the use of "the great state of Texas,"
always heard at political conventions, or the exhortation by those running for office to "keep America great." Greatness remains a part of the
mind-set of those wanting to honor teaching in the same ceremonial and
even juvenile sense that greatness is given as a value to motivate the
American population. It remains associated with elitism, with a sense of
winning an imaginary worldwide competition for being "number one,"
the very value seen at hundreds of sports events regularly, hysterically
chanted by large crowds in the United States.

   While Boyer's own language is reasonable and appealing, here is how
he presents one of his most important recommendations about teaching
in universities:

> To expect faculty to be good teachers, as well as good researchers, is
> to set a demanding standard. Still, it is at the research university,
> more than any other, where the two must come together. To bring
> teaching and research into better balance, we urge the nation's
> ranking universities to extend special status and salary incentives to
> those professors who devote most of their time to teaching and are
> particularly effective in the classroom. Such recognition will signify
> that the campus regards teaching excellence as a hallmark of profes-
> sional success. (58)

The conventional sense of this paragraph is its endorsement of the
joining of teaching and research, which, in part, it is. Nevertheless,
consider the following: Should the nation's "ranking universities" be
singled out? (Statements like this convert the mere listing of categories
of postsecondary schools into a "ranking.") Is it their special responsibility to provide leadership? An alternative formulation might read: "The
nation's research universities might seek guidance from other universities about what they have learned from their long attention to teaching."
This would strike quite a different note, set a different pace, and provide
support for the depriviliging of the system of ranking.

   "Special status and salary incentives": This phrase continues the
singling out process with its attention to status as well as the association
of status with salary, an association that helps to define the academic
pyramid. In addition, it assumes a special "incentive" is required for this
project, perhaps an allusion to the profit motive which maintains the

economic pyramid in the rest of society. But suppose, rather, the statement read: "Those in research universities should find out how many among them have been devoting equal time to teaching and research, how many have integrated them, how these people's professional welfare has progressed, and then invite them to help others toward these goals." While Boyer may not disagree with my restatement, it nevertheless strikes less of a behavioral engineering note and bypasses the casually presented presumption that status and reward are the only paths to social change because those are what everyone seeks.

"Effective in the classroom." Effectiveness is yet another taken-for-granted term used about teaching, resembling a similarly suspicious phrase, "good in bed." (Is it the case that sexual performance is a purely individual matter, independent of the partnership necessarily associated with sexual activity?) In the same sense that sexual performance is only one aspect of maintaining a relationship, effectiveness in the classroom cannot be equated with teaching and is, anyway, a relative value. In many courses, particularly large lecture courses, effectiveness has to do with the ability to hold the attention of large numbers of students, and the quality of teaching is identified with and assumed to be the performance value of the lecturer. While Boyer's phrase is not intrinsically offensive, it nevertheless fails to address the matter of the ongoing *teaching relationship* among teachers and students and seems to call most attention to the *performance* of teachers in the classroom on a class-by-class basis. "Effectiveness" is not a term which can describe a human relationship, but rather, a successful instrumentality, not necessarily human, as in "effective birth control techniques succeed in preventing pregnancy"; but one would not say "an 'effective' love relationship is one which lasts." Because teaching entails a living human relationship, using the term "effective" to describe it suggests that there is a distinct impoverishment of vocabulary, even in common parlance, when we try to articulate what people want from teaching relationships. Instead of "effective in the classroom," one could alternatively say "deeply involved in all forms of teaching." As a substantive experience, involvement matters more in teaching than effectiveness, which implies that there is a fixed and measurable result of good teaching.

"Teaching excellence as a hallmark of professional success." "Excellence" may be the academic version of the term "greatness" that we find in more popular venues. Few people have the vocabulary to question this term, since, under the rules of today's academic ideology, to question excellence is something like advocating flag burning. Yet this term, which in some sense does play a role in the thinking of most of us, carries with it some of the athletic meanings referring to achieving at a level *better than all others.* To excel is to be the best *as compared with others.* Again, few question the state of mind which urges everyone to be the best. Yet this value is extremely distant from the value of *doing one's best,* which does not imply comparing oneself to others. Buried in the public sense of the term "excellence" are the tropes and rituals of competition as well as the sense that the quality of one's work reaches its proper destination only when it is *measured,* a value overtly endorsed by the Boyer report. Those of us who take teaching seriously know that this is usually false about teaching: measurement may tell us when we have achieved the right level of automobile safety, but it will not identify when good teaching is going on. We do not and ought not to strive for "excellence" in the sense of outdoing others or even winning a prize. Rather, we do and ought to strive for reaching our students, for creating an atmosphere of stimulation, excitement, activity, and motivation. We ought to reject the claim that such values can only be assured by a final system of measurement. If teachers who are actually striving for something like "vitality" in teaching situations are distracted by the competitive feeling that they must become excellent according to some system of judgment, there will no longer be any reason to take risks in the service of vitality: there will only be reasons to accommodate the system. The fundamental fact that teaching purposes, styles, and needs are changing at every moment will be lost in the teachers' efforts to create the excellence that has been already achieved by either themselves or others, instead of trying to become responsive to the ever-changing population of students coming into our classrooms. It is much easier and more likely to expect vitality than excellence in teaching, especially because few will seek to measure vitality and involvement, while it is assumed that excellence is something that can be measured and assessed.

But suppose the term "involvement" were substituted for "assessment": self-involvement, peer involvement, teacher and mutual involvement. Wouldn't the resulting terms then necessarily refer to the substance and daily activity of teaching, rather than imply that the teaching is done first and then "techniques" are used to evaluate it? Similarly, if the *idea* of involvement more generally took the place of measurement and assessment, wouldn't the process of evaluation and self-evaluation become an ongoing, internalized aspect of all teaching? In fact, if one consults the informal conversations of serious, dedicated teachers on a daily basis, isn't it true that they share with one another, regardless of what formal evaluation systems exist, what works and what doesn't work? What worked last year and not this year? What works with this population and not that? Furthermore, if the idea of involvement is seen from an ideological perspective, it applies as well to how research is evaluated. Research can be understood as being involved with other aspects of an individual's professional life rather than as an isolated zone of achievement. Pursuant to the ideal of "taking pride in [one's] uniqueness" (Boyer 1990, xiii), an individual's research could possibly be viewed as part of other categories of effort, forming for that person a characteristic means of contribution to local or national communities or both:

> When it comes to pulling all the evidence together, we are impressed by the *portfolio* idea—a procedure that encourages faculty to document their work in a variety of ways. A faculty member could choose the form of scholarship around which a portfolio might be developed. The material used could include many of the varied forms we've described—ranging from publications, to fieldwork documentation, to course descriptions, peer reviews, student evaluations, and even, perhaps, recordings and videocassettes. (Boyer 1990, 40–41)

Except for its invocation of and commitment to the need for "vigorous assessment," this report does help to point things in an authentically new direction: the direction of unifying the professional program of individual faculty members. But the more that remediation and assessment are promoted, the less likely it is that a new direction will be realized.

The writing program at Syracuse University has tried to move in this new direction. Among the various examples it cites, the Carnegie report specifically mentions this program, which developed, in December 1989, new specific criteria for promotion and tenure in that program. The document (written by Louise Wetherbee Phelps and others) in which these criteria are spelled out (Syracuse University et al. 1989) points to the following issue not raised by Boyer: *the specificity of teaching relative to the discipline and subject matter.* On the one hand, the wider-ranging criteria for conceptualizing teaching in Boyer's report make it easier to particularize what teaching is in each subject matter. At the same time, in spite of his endorsement of the portfolio approach, Boyer retains a sense that teaching as an issue may be separated from other university enterprises such as research and service, a common view in almost all universities. On the other hand, the Syracuse guidelines, only a small part of which are cited, do demonstrate the particular meaning of teaching as it relates to the subject matter of writing and language use. The Syracuse guidelines, like Boyer's report, move far toward changing the idea of teaching toward one in which the evaluation of it is more benign and naturalistic while less controlling and hierarchical than it is now. Here is a general statement of how the Syracuse writing program treats teaching:

> We interpret teaching broadly as contributions to the educational
> enterprise, necessarily but not exclusively with the program and
> university. Activities under this heading include individual class-
> room teaching; tutoring and acting as a program writing consultant
> (to other writing teachers, classes, students, faculty in other disci-
> plines); co-teaching with others; supervising independent study
> projects; advising; arranging and supervising internships; serving
> on graduate examination and thesis, dossier, or dissertation com-
> mittees; mentoring other teachers; and leading or participating in
> workshops and co-curricular projects. In addition, teaching in-
> cludes course and curriculum development work and the design
> and implementation of professional development for teaching as-
> sistants and professional instructors in writing. Finally, teaching
> includes an array of nontraditional roles in writing across the
> curriculum, for example, offering workshops or acting as an advisor
> to teaching assistants in other disciplines. (Syracuse University et al.
> 1989, 4)

If all of these activities are eligible for inclusion in a teaching portfolio,
it is clear that evaluation in the sense of measurement is far in the
background and perhaps altogether out of the picture. The portfolio
technique tries to show that different forms of teaching are connected to
one another in a kind of program or style. It assumes that *every* teacher
teaches in a variety of styles and contexts, in addition to the classroom.

Also especially noteworthy is the tailoring of the concept of teaching
to the subject matter of writing. As Louise Phelps, one of the authors of
the Syracuse guidelines, has discussed, composition, as a subject in
itself, should be considered an academic discipline. Those of us in the
writing business take this for granted. One of the distinctive features of
this discipline is its demand for various approaches to teaching, such as
tutoring and curriculum design, collaborative work, and portfolio
evaluation. As suggested by the Syracuse guidelines, the discipline
itself *requires* a wide-ranging alertness on the part of all writing teachers
to special combinations of literacy theory and teaching practice, a point
further elaborated on by Phelps (1991) in an essay in *College English*. As
discussed in the Boyer report, we still too often get the sense that
teaching practices are similar across subject matter disciplines and *do
not need* to be conceptualized per department, per discipline, per university, per teacher, and even per student. On the other hand, a clear
implication of the Syracuse guidelines is that just as teaching has a
distinctive identity when it comes to the discipline of writing, it also has
different identities within that program and for that program, identities
which may not fit other universities and other programs. In any event,
the shift toward portfolio evaluation does finally engage the ideological
dimension of evaluation itself, whether it is applied to student writing

or to the teaching of writing. In particular, it shifts the idea of evaluation into a discourse of particularization, to standards of "local knowledge," to needs, values, and purposes of local school and university situations, as well as to the requirements of different disciplines. In part, the Boyer report does advocate this change, but more is involved in such a change than is discussed in the report.

To get a sense of what this "more" might be, I present, here, a journal extract by one of Wendy Bishop's graduate students, presented in one of Bishop's recent essays (Bishop 1991):

> The portfolio system is not designed to check up on the TA's, it is designed to promote the concept of the TA as coach, not evaluator. The place where this concept falls apart is that I grade all my papers, as do, I think, all or most of the other TA's. So the concept of TA as coach and peer can only go so far. And in any case, the TA has to give the final class grade.
>
> I cannot see any alternative to grading each particular paper. My students would go ape-s— without grades. I will also admit that I would have trouble keeping track of how each student was doing in terms of final grade[s] without some sort of paper to paper grading system. —Steve (215)

[Evaluators: Should we worry about the comma splice in the first sentence of the preceding extract?] This student, not surprisingly male, welcomes the relief portfolio evaluation provides for him but feels he cannot meet his responsibility to the system. By contrast, here is the comment of a female TA in the pedagogy seminar described by Bishop:

> I am so pleased. Everyone of my students got in his or her portfolio and arrived to class on time. What a wonderful feeling; I was so proud of them.... I read the midterm self-evaluations that they wrote in class yesterday. I'm impressed by the fact that they really do know what grade each of them probably deserves and will probably get. They all seemed very close. [If s]ome were a little harder on themselves than I would be I think they're impressed with the work they've done. Some feel that their portfolio draft is the best paper they've ever written. Many of them were also actually surprised by the difference between the first rough draft and the portfolio draft ... Monday was a very good day. —Peg (215–16)

Although Bishop does not make this point explicitly, the two responses to portfolio evaluation may be read as gender coded. Let me read them in a somewhat unorthodox way. Steve's comment concerned his sense of himself; Peg's described how the students felt. Steve commented on his responsibility to evaluate each paper. Peg commented on the students' evaluation of one another's essays. Steve reported on where the concept "falls apart" and does not announce his feelings; Peg comments on the "wonderful feeling" she had as a result of her students' full participation and involvement. Steve is concerned with "keeping track" of the students; Peg is concerned with the students being too hard on one another. It only takes the listing of these differences to tease out a tacit point in Bishop's epilogic citation. Beneath the actual practice of portfolio evaluation are ideological orientations that are not that distantly related to cultural gender identity.

In an essay in the same volume, Cheryl Armstrong Smith's (1991) argument for "Writing without Testing" cites three "questions repeatedly . . . asked about portfolios at [her] university": plagiarism, students' independent performance, and consistent standards. She characterizes these questions as all raising "issues of authority and control. They are not questions about whether or not we are actually measuring writing abilities" (287). If we do not treat issues of authority and control as functions of people's wish for personal power, they can be understood as invocations of the traditional academic ideology whose highest ideals entail the individual pursuit of excellence—that is, without help, covert or overt, from others but competing with them—and an utterly and, if possible, mathematically uniform technique of "measuring" this excellence. Smith rejects "ranking writing" and advocates the abandonment of exit testing altogether:

> The subtext of the three questions I found most frequently asked about portfolios seems to be that the purpose of exit testing is to provide an external, higher authority to check up on teachers or to check up on students. . . . By using portfolios but abandoning exit tests in writing programs, we would acknowledge that teachers are authorities about the work taking place in their own classrooms, that collaboration encourages the development of writing ability and of effective teaching, and that learning to write is not a matter of passing tests but is a lifelong process. (291)

Smith identifies and explains the point raised by Steve in his journal entry: he understood that the portfolio system was "not designed" to check up on teachers. But he did not write that it is "designed" to function *under a completely new ideology.* It is not likely that he addressed the ideological function of the portfolio system, since he reports in the same passage both on how he cannot see how his own responsibilities would be met without going through the traditional one-to-one grading process, and he guesses that his students would be completely disoriented if he did.

Even though people (myself included) do give grades to total portfolios as a reasonable first step away from constant judging and grading, the *ideology* of portfolio evaluation is incommensurate with that of individual grading. Steve's disorientation comes from his experience of incommensurability as well as his gender stake in the traditional deployment of classroom authority and control, which he describes as "keeping track" of the work of each student. In fact, Steve felt that, regardless of the new space opened up by a portfolio approach, he must finally return to the style of responsible teaching in which the teacher has a dyadic relationship with each student and where grades are assigned *per student* in comparison with one another (de facto competition). In spite of his perception of the lack of checking up, he does not accord it enough importance to have it imply that, perhaps, he must *not* finally return to the authoritative giving of the grade. This happens partly because ideology itself cannot be taught or inculcated directly. Whatever Steve may learn ideologically must be the result of his learning *from his own work environment*, which may include peers, teachers, students, university rules, everything that reflects ideological identification. Seen otherwise, Steve's political position now prevents him from overtaking, in its ideological dimension, what Bishop brought to the class. His achievement has been mainly to acknowledge more than one view: "I felt lucky to have instructors/mentors that *do not* have the same views. I figure a good balance can be struck" (Bishop 1991, 224).

Peg does not report a divided frame of mind. In the preceding and in another extract from her comments, she expresses support for the portfolio system and for its collective oversight: a team of readers, the TAs and two faculty members, judged each portfolio for pass or not-pass status. Her remarks suggest that she views the portfolio evaluation and the changes in classroom social relations it provided without a sense of contradiction and without an underlying ideological dissonance. Because of the collective approach to grading, where grades were discussed by three people before being assigned, Peg had no problem leaving the traditional grading style behind. While grading itself is still a part of the demand to rank the students, the new social relations of the class overrode this factor for her, and she reported that complete success, in terms of all work being completed by everyone, was achieved.

Peg's political perspective and position must already have been more receptive to the paradigmatic ideology of process teaching and portfolio evaluation. That this ideology may be gender affiliated is suggested by the difference in reporting, presented above, between her comments and Steve's. She is already student oriented, or perhaps, she already thinks of herself as part of a collective scene, someone who is responsible not for keeping track of others, but for their good feeling and sense of accomplishment. She felt responsible for the subjective welfare of the students rather than for a complete account of their performance. To some, it may not be obvious that the difference between Peg and Steve is one between gender-identified ideologies. Yet it would be fair to say that the issues raised in the Carnegie report about teaching and research are not that far from the issues raised by the two senses of teaching represented by Steve and Peg. A fundamental question about teaching is also a fundamental question about gender ideology and gender roles.

The second chapter of Madeleine Grumet's *Bitter Milk: Women and Teaching* (1988) is entitled "Pedagogy for Patriarchy: The Feminization of Teaching." This chapter, as well as other aspects of her book, provides a historical background for the differences between Steve and Peg as well as for the different voices in the Boyer report. (For example, the voice calling for more assessment of teaching as opposed to the voice calling for status independence). This background helps us to view both sets of differences as belonging to problems of gender ideology, of which the ideology of competition may be considered a part, as the contributors to the Miner and Longino (1987) volume suggest. Grumet reviews some of the nineteenth-century history of school development in America. After detailing how men held the vast majority of administrative jobs in education throughout the nineteenth century, Grumet offers the following thought:

> Horace Mann's preference for female teachers and an ideal of gentle, loving influence was a reaction against the hard Calvinism of Nathanael Emmons, the powerful minister of his boyhood. Associating Emmons's severity with pure intellect, Mann preferred to match the "milk and gentle manners of women to the tenderness of childhood." It is possible that the feminization of teaching was originally located at the crossroads of masculine and feminine projects to rectify their own object relations. Cut off from their mothers by the harsh masculine authority of church and fathers, theorists like Mann sought the reclamation of mother love by promoting women as teachers of the young. Overwhelmed by the presence of their mothers, women entered teaching in order to gain access to the power and prerogatives of their fathers. (54)

I will take two thoughts from this analysis of Mann's bringing female teachers into the schools. First, I get a historical sense that a not-wholly-narcissistic gender psychology could be found in male educators, but that it was clearly a gender psychology with some connections to today's gender psychology; and second, I get the sense that at least some distinct affirmative value was placed by men and women on the female-identified characteristics of nurturance. This value served both men and women, historically and personally. Grumet implies that men found Calvinistic severity burdensome, much as, perhaps, they find military, corporate, and athletic psychology burdensome today; they therefore would support a consistent and sensible way to make school more flexible and responsive to the turns of juvenile social psychology. Certainly today, everyone in school would like to find disciplined ways to practice in school the home-derived sense of relaxation within rules of decency and courtesy. Most would want school to be the site of enjoyment, feeling, and the celebration of learning. At the same time, women who became teachers (wanting, as Grumet describes, to identify with their fathers) sought recognition for their ability and desire to teach in a "nurturance" mode. To hold the job was itself a partial accession to the authority of the men who hired them. Grumet thus describes this historical development as a kind of psychosocial trade with advantages for each gender as they were then culturally identified.

But, of course, there continued to exist a superstructure of society— the enduring pyramid cited by Longino in her description of the trip from feudal to bourgeois society (1987, 253). Because of this continuing structure, gender inequality was perpetuated in schools, as Grumet describes:

> So male educators invited women into the schools expecting to reclaim their mothers, and the women accepted the invitation and came so that they might identify with their fathers. Accordingly, female teachers complied with the rationalization and the bureaucratization that pervaded the common schools as the industrial culture saturated the urban areas. Rather than emulate the continuous and extended relations of a mother and her maturing child, they acquiesced to the graded schools—to working with one age group for one year at a time. Rather than demand the extended relation that would bind them over time to individual children, they agreed to large group instruction where the power of the peer collective was at least as powerful as the mother/child bond. Deprived of the classical education that most of the males who organized the schools enjoyed, normalites accepted the curriculum as bestowed, and deviations from it remained in the privacy of the classroom and were not presented to principals or committees of visitors. (Grumet 1988, 55)

In short, it was not finally a fair exchange. Because female styles and standards were already considered secondary and inferior, they were suppressed, and women themselves were not permitted growth, expression, and authority. Grumet shows that the features of school we now consider commonplace and "normal" were culturally coerced by the condition of gender inequality during the period of industrialization. She implies that under more egalitarian conditions, we might now be seeing students of different ages in a single classroom, a variable curriculum, perhaps geared to the differing student populations; continuing, carried-over relationships between students and teachers over long periods of time; the presence and use of the peer collective but not its hegemony of style and demand; and finally, a free exchange of ideas and response between teachers and school administrators. These latter values need not be gender identified. But as Grumet recounts this phase of the history of education in the United States, that has been their fate. And because of this identification, they have been suppressed, to the detriment of society.

One more item before relating Grumet's account to our interrogation of teaching in today's postsecondary writing programs: the fragmenting of women's interests and the further consolidation of control over education by established masculine-defined forces:

> Furthermore, the gender contradictions, the simultaneous assertion and denial of femininity, have served to estrange teachers of children and the mothers of those children. Instead of being allies, mothers and teachers distrust each other. Bearing credentials of a profession that claimed the colors of motherhood and then systematically delivered the children over to the language, rules, and relations of the patriarchy, teachers understandably feel uneasy, mothers suspicious. Their estrangement leaves a gap in school governance that the professional administrators, the state, and textbook publishers rush in to fill. Until teachers and mothers acknowledge the ways in which schools perpetuate the asymmetry in class privilege and gender that is present in both the home and the workplace, they will not interrupt the patterns of their own complicity. (Grumet 1988, 56)

Parents and teachers are, in part, adversarially related to one another. While Grumet is emphasizing this opposition in earlier schooling, where both mothers and female teachers are more in the picture, teaching remains "feminized," relative to research, in the university. Masculine cultural psychology being in strong evidence in the academy, teaching and learning within the university are depersonalized and diminished in value as well as distanced from parents, who participate in university life mainly through the payment of tuition. While faculty have a voice in determining the curriculum, it too is depersonalized by the fact that a faculty member's research agenda, as the Boyer report notes, is usually distant from the subject matter of the courses taught by that faculty member. If one entertains this sense of a gap between faculty/research and students/teaching, it could also be seen as void in governance: neither parents nor faculty members actually govern a university. This gap is not filled but widened by administrators, by the state, by the board of trustees, on which are almost always representatives of corporate America, and by textbook publishers, who are often seen in university halls and professional conventions persuading faculty to use their wares. All of these interests represent socially masculine values and styles as well as the ideology of competition and hierarchy. Teachers in the university are "feminized" in the sense described by Grumet. It is this circumstance that makes the Carnegie report germane. But it is also the reason that this report devoted no space at all to conceiving the "problem" of teaching as a problem of gender ideology. If it had, it might have relied less prominently on appeals to the search for excellence and on the redoubled call for assessments of all kinds of all activities.

If teaching is feminized in the academy, then the teaching of writing is even more feminized. Susan Miller, in her recent treatise *Textual Carnivals: The Politics of Composition* (1991), characterized the majority of writing teachers as "the sad women in the basement." This phrase refers to the fact that most teachers of writing are female, either adjunct or untenured, occupying the lowest rung on the academic ladder, but as a whole are the largest faculty group in the academy and the ones reaching the most students most often—again a situation that corresponds to Grumet's description of teachers in schools. The Boyer report might very well have mentioned that the Syracuse writing program took the initiatives it did with regard to tenure and promotion guidelines because it had a female directorate which separated the program from departmental oversight. While such separation may not be the right step in other universities and may raise additional problems, there is no denying that in the case of Syracuse, it is an achievement of autonomy that points up the political difficulties in most other writing programs—mainly, their reduced status in the university at large. At Syracuse, the separation created a venue for the articulation of new academic values, recognized as such by Boyer.

If only parenthetically, but to suggest resonance of the Syracuse issue with problems in other communities, I would like to call attention to what happened to the writing program at the University of Texas. Again with a female director, Linda Brodkey, the proposed writing program was politically bolder than the one at Syracuse, explicitly relating the teaching of writing to national political debates. It remained under the oversight of the English department, but it won the support of a large majority of that department. Once it became clear that this program would be enacted, a minority of the department, many of whom were affiliated with the neoconservative National Association of Scholars, appealed to university authority, beyond even the dean of the college, and succeeded in blocking even its temporary or experimental implementation. Because of overarching ideological forces at the University of Texas, it is hard to say that Brodkey's program would have been tried even if there was an autonomous writing program.

In this climate for the teaching of writing, we cannot seriously entertain the matter of evaluation of teaching without engaging directly the constituency that is asking for evaluation. The *premise* that teaching *requires* evaluation itself is in need of discussion. On the other hand, if we advocate for continuous evaluation embedded in a flexible, interactive, intersubjective curricular approach to writing, this implies that we are to be affiliated with an entirely different paradigm, a different ideology of teaching and research in the academy. The Boyer report is only partially consistent with such a shift, as it took pains to minimize in its vocabulary any discussion of such controversial matters as gender or minority ideology.

A different paradigm for teaching writing involves, of course, the use of portfolios and collaborative work in the classroom. But as Steve noted, these alone will not enact or realize change, though they represent a beginning. The most palpable obstacle to change is the stubborn presence of the ideology of competitive individualism and its need for ranking and hierarchical structures in the academy. Its signs are the obsession with grades and the need for "checking up" on those below by those above. It is clear, on the other hand, that classrooms such as Peg's can flourish even though the environment is not particularly sympathetic. We do not know what went on in Peg's classroom, what her style was like, what her curriculum proposed. But it is nevertheless clear that the curriculum itself must be joined substantively with the involved and intersubjective styles of teaching which would include as a matter of course all kinds of evaluation and particularly different forms of self-evaluation. A curriculum that is critical of society can also be critical of itself. Students and teachers who are involved with one another can be thoughtfully critical of one another and will eventually become students and teachers of one another. When members of classrooms feel that involvement is more fundamental than assessment, the many directions of teaching and learning will be enjoyed by all.

Every act of writing involves a choice of vocabulary, a tone, a voice, a judgment, and most important, an appeal, a call, a shout, or an invitation of some sort to other people. Grumet calls this human dimension of writing the "phenomenology of the familiar": the sense that a choice of words is necessarily an invocation of human feeling, aesthetic, dramatic, perhaps unconscious, and always interpersonal. To admit these dimensions to the forefront of writing is also to admit them to the forefront of teaching. To admit them into the academy is to change the usual meanings of teaching, writing, and research. It is to recognize the new demographies of the classroom as well as the necessary involvement of the phenomenology of the familiar with the ideology of enfranchisement. Perhaps terms like "phenomenology" and "ideology" are already gender identified. But if we can raise such issues of language and public life in our classrooms, we will be teaching writing and teaching teaching.

Works Cited

Bishop, Wendy. 1991. "Going up the Creek without a Canoe: Using Portfolios to Train New Teachers of College Writing." In *Portfolios: Process and Product*, edited by Pat Belanoff and Marcia Dickson, 215–28. Portsmouth, NH: Boynton/Cook.

Boyer, Ernest L. 1990. *Scholarship Reconsidered: Priorities of the Professoriate*. Princeton, NJ: The Carnegie Foundation for the Advancement of Teaching.

Grumet, Madeleine R. 1988. *Bitter Milk: Women and Teaching*. Amherst: University of Massachusetts Press.

Longino, Helen E. 1987. "The Ideology of Competition." In *Competition: A Feminist Taboo?* edited by Valerie Miner and Helen E. Longino, 248–58. New York: The Feminist Press.

Miller, Susan. 1991. *Textual Carnivals: The Politics of Composition*. Carbondale: Southern Illinois University Press.

Ong, Walter, J. 1981. *Fighting for Life: Contest, Sexuality, and Consciousness*. Ithaca: Cornell University Press.

Phelps, Louise Wetherbee. 1991. "Practical Wisdom and the Geography of Knowledge in Composition." *College English* 53: 863–85.

Smith, Cheryl Armstrong. 1991. "Writing without Testing." In *Portfolios: Process and Product*, edited by Pat Belanoff and Marcia Dickson, 279–92. Portsmouth, NH: Boynton/Cook.

Syracuse University, Louise Wetherbee Phelps, and others. 1989. "The Writing Program Promotion and Tenure Guidelines." Syracuse, NY: University of Syracuse.

3 Evaluating College Teaching: An Overview

Jesse Jones
University of North Texas

If Chaucer's Clerk were a modern college writing instructor seeking promotion at an American equivalent of Southwark Community College or Canterbury U., a written affirmation that "He gladly learns, and gladly teaches" from chairperson Chaucer's classroom visit would be helpful.

But if the Clerk's institution is typical, additional information would be required before a decision were to be made. How about his service to the department, the institution, the community? What do his student evaluations reveal? What has he published? To provide answers to these and other questions, there would be in place a faculty evaluation process, a process which more than likely would have progressed through various stages over the previous several years.

> In the 1960s . . . the evaluation of teaching . . . was in good part a response to student demands for public accountability and for a voice in governance. . . . In the 1970s, a more gentle use of evaluation was touted. . . . Self-assessment, study, and development were aided by objective information about one's performance. This was a peak period for the growth of campus instructional and faculty development units. In the 1980s, however, management has been faced with a need for objective data in making tough administrative decisions. (Geis 1984, 106)

And if the Clerk's college is not just typical but exemplary, the results of those decades of change will work to his benefit:

> the entire evaluation process is becoming more structured and systematic. More data sources are being introduced, and the assessment procedures are more open . . . Other data sources—classroom visits, course syllabi and examinations, and self-evaluation—are emerging in importance. (Seldin 1984, 73–74)

> In the time I have been an observer of faculty evaluation, I have seen it steadily move to more care in gathering data, more attention to ruling out prejudice and subjectivity, and more involvement of those actually affected by the process. (Eble 1984, 96)

If, indeed, the Clerk's college has reached the point Seldin and Eble describe, it will have done so by spending a great deal of time, energy, and money over the years in addressing and answering questions such as the following:

> Should we be evaluating teaching? If so, what is our purpose?
>
> What do we evaluate?
>
> What sources and types of data do we use?
>
> What are the characteristics of an effective evaluation process? How do we measure our effectiveness?
>
> What is the appropriate metaphor that should govern and direct our evaluation of one another as teachers?

What follow are brief summaries of the dialogue that has taken place among college faculty and administrators regarding each of these questions, quotations from key contributors to the discussions, indications of where we are currently, and a few observations of my own.

Should We Be Evaluating Teaching?

In considering this most fundamental of questions, some of us have disagreed philosophically with the need for—have even disputed the possibility of—formal assessment of classroom teaching: "To intimidate teachers by threatening them with formal evaluation is to discourage experimentation in teaching, and thus to deprive both students and citizens of that very excellence in professional service which a system of evaluation is meant to secure" (Larson 1970, 9).

Others of us have agreed that evaluation is needed, but have expressed a preference for an informal, self-directed model: "Isn't it true that if student critiques were a part of the teaching process but not a potential element in someone's judgment of us from 'above,' we teachers would all be much more eager to hear them, as well as to take them seriously?" (Bleich 1992, 11). And virtually all of us have had serious concerns about some facet of the current process on our campuses: "I feel quite safe in saying that very few institutions are making good use of their faculty evaluation systems for development purposes" (Aubrecht 1984, 88).

Today on campus, we may continue internally to debate the "Should we?" question of faculty evaluation, but the external public's voices and votes are all affirmative—not only for faculty evaluation, but also for overall institutional evaluation: "Increasingly, higher education's various publics—students, parents, legislators, and others—are insisting that teaching be assessed seriously and substantively" (Cashin 1990, 89). And for any institution seeking accreditation or reaccreditation, there is simply no arguing with external criteria such as the following:

> 4.4.10 *Criteria and Procedures for Evaluation*
>
> An institution must conduct periodic evaluations of the performance of individual faculty members. The evaluation must include a statement of the criteria against which the performance of each faculty member will be measured. These criteria must be made known to all concerned. The institution must demonstrate that it uses the results of this evaluation for the improvement of the faculty and the educational program. (Southern Association of Colleges and Schools 1991, 30–31)

Even in our internal dialogue, however, the discussion seems largely to have shifted from "Shall we?" to "How shall we?"—as illustrated by the essays in this volume.

What Is Our Purpose?

There are basically two reasons for evaluating faculty members. They are the same two reasons for evaluating administrators. They are the same two reasons reflected in the *"commentary* (or feedback)" and *"measurement* (or grading and ranking)" roles (Elbow 1986, 231) that faculty members exercise with students: (1) for improving performance and (2) for making personnel decisions.

A *formative* evaluation identifies perceived strengths and weaknesses of one's performance over a stipulated period of time. The individual being evaluated, often in concert with colleagues, uses information thus gained to improve future performance. The process can be very formal, very informal, or somewhere in between. In any event, the faculty member should be given maximum opportunity to shape the process. Formative evaluation is ongoing.

A *summative* evaluation also identifies perceived strengths and weaknesses of one's performance over a stipulated period of time. In this case, however, the information is used by others—usually administrators such as the department or division chair, dean, and vice president—for judging and rewarding (or not rewarding) performance. Often at stake are such crucial career matters as continued employment, a merit pay increase, promotion in rank, or tenure; for students, a grade in a course, completion of a degree, passing or failing doctoral examinations. Sometimes the judging is for the bestowing of special awards or honors such as teacher of the year; for students, perhaps a scholarship. The summative evaluation process, since there are issues of equity and legality involved, needs to be a formal process. Summative evaluation is periodic.

Often there are broader, more encompassing purposes at work. External accountability is one; another is departmental program review; others, such campuswide initiatives as assessment, institutional effectiveness, or self-study. These evaluative purposes, however, whether internally or externally driven, often overlap, and all ultimately translate for the individual (if they extend to the level of the individual) into formative or summative evaluation.

Obviously, purpose should be determined as a first step in developing an evaluation process. The answer to the question "Why are we doing this?" will dictate such matters as data collected, sources used, and distribution of results. Since most institutions will have both purposes as goals, they will probably use some of the same processes (such as student ratings) for formative and summative evaluation. If this dual-use process is structured carefully, it can conserve time and funds. But care needs to be taken to see that the purposes complement rather than conflict with one another.

What Do We Evaluate?

What are the appropriate components of teaching for evaluation—both of teaching in general and of the teaching of writing in particular? In addressing the first part of the question, Braskamp, Brandenburg, and Ory (1984) suggest three major areas:

> In general, the evaluation of instruction can be divided by its emphasis on input (What do students and teachers bring to the classroom?), process (What do teachers and students do in a course?), or product (What do students learn or accomplish in the course?). A closer look at each emphasis should reveal that effective teaching is defined differently depending on the emphasis placed on input, process, or product. (16)

Raoul Arreola (1986) also suggests three dimensions, but identifies them as (1) content expertise, (2) instructional delivery skills and characteristics, and (3) instructional design skills (8–12).

More recently, William Cashin (1990) has expanded Arreola's three dimensions into seven and has indicated for each some types of evaluative documentation:

1. Mastery of subject matter: degrees, certificates, or licenses.
2. Curriculum development: course revisions, new courses.

3. Course design: syllabi, handouts.
4. Delivery of instruction: student ratings, videotapes.
5. Assessment of instruction: graded exams, projects, or papers.
6. Availability to students: office hours.
7. Administrative requirements: turning in book orders, probation notices, grades. (92)

As these lists indicate, many of the categories of evaluation are the same for all disciplines. But in addition, each discipline has what Lee Shulman (1989) calls a "pedagogy of substance" specific to the content of the discipline itself (8). Spelling out that pedagogy of substance so that it can be recognized and incorporated into the dimensions of teaching that are evaluated is, of course, the responsibility of the faculty in the discipline.

In writing instruction, a step in that direction was taken in 1982 by the CCCC Committee on Teaching and Its Evaluation in Composition. The group observed that "most of us whose responsibility it is to evaluate the teaching of writing do so with techniques and instruments developed for other kinds of teaching" (213). Their own analysis of writing instruction yielded seven components:

> For convenience in discussing evaluation, the Committee divides the process of teaching and learning in composition into seven parts: (1) the preliminary reflection and analysis just mentioned ["We assume that as their first step teachers have accepted some theoretical framework for viewing the act of writing and the teaching of writing, and that within this framework they have defined the goals of their teaching. We further assume that as part of this step teachers have assessed where the students are when they begin the study of writing"]; (2) the planning of the curriculum and individual writing activities; (3) the successive classroom activities engaged in by teacher and student; (4) the instructional activities—not only writing and response to writing—in which instructor and students engage together outside the classroom; (5) the learning activities—especially writing—in which students engage by themselves during the course; (6) the performances—especially of writing—in which the students engage after instruction; (7) students' recollections of and feelings about their experiences. (216)

Although there have been published studies since 1982 dealing with writing programs, including extensive work on writing program evaluation such as that of Barbara Gross Davis, Michael Scriven, and Susan Thomas (1987), most deal with program evaluation processes rather than teacher-evaluation processes. The essays in this volume provide additional guidance in refining and focusing the evaluation of writing instruction.

What Sources and Types of Data Do We Use?

Potential sources of evaluative data are current students, former students, departmental colleagues, colleagues from other departments, the department or division chair, the dean, departmental or institutional statistical reports, and self-evaluation information from the teacher being evaluated. Certain sources are best for certain items of information.

Students provide an assessment of teaching skills, content and structure of the course, work load, teacher and student interactions, organization of course materials and clarity of presentation, and student advising. *Faculty peers* provide a review of teaching materials (assignments, handouts, tests, papers), mastery and currency of subject matter, original research, professional recognition, participation in the academic community, interest in and concern for teaching, and service to the nonacademic community. *Administrators* provide an appraisal of the work load and other teaching responsibilities, student course enrollment, service to the institution, and teaching improvement. *The professor* provides self-appraisal as a teacher (and as a faculty member with added academic accomplishments, student advising, committee memberships, and service to the institution and community) (Seldin 1984, 132).

Types of evaluative data frequently used to assess teaching include surveys (such as student ratings); videotapes; interviews; course materials such as syllabi, handouts, reading lists, and exams; checklists (such as classroom visitation forms); and departmental or institutional statistical reports.

With sources and with types of data, whether the evaluation is formative or summative, the crucial requisite is underscored by Kay McClenney (qtd. in Albert 1991): "Good assessment requires multiple methods, multiple approaches, multiple perspectives" (7).

How Are We Doing at _____ College?

If the teaching evaluation process in effect on your campus fits the following descriptions, you have reason to rejoice:

> Faculty evaluation should be *systematic* (organized, standardized), *comprehensive* (taking into account the wide range of responsibilities for each individual), *public* (with known criteria and procedures), and *flexible* (designed to accommodate change and take advantage of the individual's talents and capabilities as well as to serve the needs of the academic unit). (Aubrecht 1984, 86)

> flexible, comprehensive, objective, individualized, fair, and consistent with the law. (Seldin 1984, 125)

To help you evaluate your process for the presence or absence of the general characteristics listed by Aubrecht and Seldin, following are a few questions for consideration:

I. Regarding the Formative Process

Reality Check
Is the emphasis on teaching improvement in the evaluation process reflected in the actual recognition and reward system of the department and the institution?

Participation
Do senior members of the department endorse and participate in the process, or do only the donkeys? ("The lions of a department are the frequently published scholars; the donkeys spend their time and energy teaching and advising large numbers of undergraduates and are rewarded in lowly fashion, less for their teaching skill and more for their political contribution to the department's FTE" [Sheridan 1990, 166].)

Are adjunct faculty included in the process?

Perception
Is the professional development process seen as a positive, needful, ongoing activity or as an administrative encroachment which is a pain in the professorial posterior, to be endured as infrequently as possible?

Flexibility and Inclusiveness
Does the process span all levels of course instruction, freshman through graduate? Does the process include evaluation techniques for nontraditional teaching situations such as computerized instruction, self-paced instruction, telecourse instruction?

Does the process include some type of professional development contract which the faculty member can tailor to current interests and initiatives? Can the faculty member, or the faculty member and the department or division chair, determine the relative weighting of each activity?

If survey instruments and forms contain a core of common questions, is there opportunity for the individual instructor to select and include additional questions that address areas of his or her concern?

Does the process encourage experimentation, innovation, creativity? Does it foster interest and research in cultural diversity and student learning styles? Does it place a premium on collaborative efforts by faculty colleagues, activities such as mentoring, classroom visitations, team teaching within the department and between departments, working with colleagues who are experts in curriculum development, test construction, computerized instruction, educational technology, multimedia, overall teaching improvement?

Sources and Types of Information

Are the appropriate people asked the appropriate questions? Are questions on the student survey instrument, for example, limited to those areas students can be expected to know something about and about which they can provide valuable information?

Is opportunity provided students and others for written observations? If so, is the student's anonymity and safety from reprisal protected in the way in which and at the time at which the information is shared with the faculty member?

Are several sources and several types of data included?

Are the questions on the survey instruments detailed and diagnostic rather than general?

Follow-through

Does the program, department or division, and institution provide adequate, systematic assistance for the faculty member to pursue improvements in specific areas of teaching based on evaluative findings? (To repeat an earlier quotation: "I feel quite safe in saying that very few institutions are making good use of their faculty evaluation systems for development purposes" [Aubrecht 1984, 88].)

II. Regarding the Summative Process

Reality Check

Will teaching and demonstrated improvement in teaching be given sufficient weight in awarding promotion or tenure? Is the junior faculty member well advised to devote time and energy to teaching research and improvement as well as traditional research and publication?

To what extent is the summative evaluation process applied during the initial hiring of a faculty member? How much attention is given to teaching? Is a teaching portfolio or the equivalent (with sample syllabi, handouts, exams, student ratings) required as part of the application? Is a teaching demonstration required as part of the interview process, with current faculty members being asked to use classroom evaluation forms and techniques? Do interview questions include questions about teaching philosophy, teaching style, teaching experience?

Communication
In the case of tenure or extended-contract evaluation, does the process include guidance and counsel for the candidate in case the decision is a negative one? That is, does the process help the candidate understand future career options and possibilities in case he or she is not granted tenure?

In the case of tenure or extended-contract evaluation, are the results of the decision and the reasons for that decision conveyed to the candidate along with the decision itself?

Fairness and Equity
On the survey instruments and forms used, is there a core set of questions and criteria that are applied in all departments to all candidates undergoing review? Is there an opportunity for the faculty member being evaluated to select additional questions for inclusion and to include additional documentation?

III. Regarding Both Processes

Communication
Are all procedures in writing? Are they shared in advance with those participating in the process?

Are all evaluative criteria in writing? Are they shared in advance with those participating in the process?

Is it made clear to all involved, including students, whether the process is for professional development, personnel decision making, or both?

Is it made clear to all involved, including students, who will get what evaluative information?

Is information gathered for teaching improvement purposes shared only with the faculty member and others directly involved?

Complementary Fit
Do the evaluative criteria and overall processes reflect the goals and needs of the individual, the program, the department or division, and the college?

Are the processes part of an overall integrated system of formative and summative employee evaluations for all employee classifications?

Are the evaluation processes an integral part of the planning and budgeting processes of the program, department or division, and college?

Does the recognition and reward system of the program, department or division, and college support the processes?

Resources
Are the time and energy demanded on the part of all who participate, including students, within reason? ("In general, a crucial fact of faculty evaluation is that the more rigorous it becomes, the more it creates a desire [in] the faculty to play a strong part, and the greater become the demands on faculty members' time" [Eble 1984, 98].)

Can the department and the institution adequately support the process with staffing and funding as necessary?

Ownership
Have faculty members been largely responsible for developing and refining the processes so that there is a real sense of ownership and control?

Sensitivity
Do the processes recognize and are they sensitive to normal human anxieties, concerns, and defensiveness regarding evaluation (whether the person being evaluated is a faculty member, a secretary, or a dean)? ("The human side of evaluation is crucial. Evaluation of persons is a deeply personal and sensitive undertaking. We have yet to work with someone who has not been anxious, interested, or concerned about an assessment of his or her work" [Braskamp, Brandenburg, and Ory 1984, 12].)

Preparation and Training
Is appropriate training provided for special activities such as portfolio preparation, classroom observation, preparation of a professional development contract?

Evaluation
Are there regular reviews of the evaluation processes?

If you answered "no" an uncomfortable number of times, and if you agree that "yes" is the appropriate answer in each case, then your process needs overhauling. There are, for that purpose, noteworthy how-to works—beginning, of course, with this volume. Those sources I have found most helpful include Richard Larson's *The Evaluation of Teaching College English* (1970); the CCCC Committee on Teaching and Its Evaluation in Composition's "Evaluating Instruction in Writing: Approaches and Instruments" (1982); Larry Braskamp, Dale Brandenburg, and John Ory's *Evaluating Teaching Effectiveness: A Practical Guide* (1984); Peter Seldin's *Changing Practices in Faculty Evaluation: A Critical Assessment and Recommendations for Improvement* (1984); Richard Miller's *Evaluating Faculty for Promotion and Tenure* (1987); Lawrence Aleamoni's *Techniques for Evaluating and Improving Instruction* (1987); Barbara Gross Davis, Michael Scriven, and Susan Thomas's *The Evaluation of Composition Instruction* (1987); and Peter Seldin and Associates' *How Administrators Can Improve Teaching: Moving from Talk to Action in Higher Education* (1990).

What Is the Appropriate Metaphor for Evaluating Teaching?

In their article "Avoiding Mixed Metaphors of Faculty Evaluation," Rodney Riegle and Dent Rhodes (1986) begin their discussion with this paragraph:

> The language of faculty evaluation is riddled with vagueness and ambiguity. The inevitable results include unproductive research and ineffective policies. Consequently, those conducting evaluations are often unsure as to how to proceed or they proceed in undesirable and even contradictory ways. There seem to be at least five different metaphors of evaluation: judging, critiquing, assessing, appraising, rating. Of course, these metaphors sometimes overlap, but nevertheless it is possible to distinguish among them. Each of these metaphors can significantly affect the way one thinks and acts when engaged in evaluating. (123)

Operant metaphors do indeed "significantly affect the way one thinks and acts when engaged in evaluating." And while the metaphors listed are those often associated with faculty evaluation and evaluation in general, there are others which Riegle and Rhodes do not mention, metaphors which suggest a different attitude and approach.

Much of the metaphorical ambiguity in faculty evaluation stems from our failure to distinguish clearly—in our language and in our processes of evaluation—between its formative and summative purposes. As Peter Elbow (1986) notes, "'Evaluation' refers to two very different activities: *measurement* (or grading or ranking) and *commentary* (or feedback)" (231). In context, of course, he is referring to the evaluation of students by writing teachers. But the purposes he identifies, with changes in terminology, are the same as those for evaluating faculty. Evaluators are trying, on the one hand, to improve performance (provide commentary or feedback); they are required, on the other hand, to render judgments (grading and ranking).

Elbow's observation is from the teacher's perspective. To further illustrate the point, I have reproduced the following comment from an administrator. In brackets, I have added suggested shifts in wording that stress, again, the similarity of situations:

> I was asked to write this piece from the point of view of a departmental chair [faculty member] and to consider the tensions between the roles of nurturer and judge and between the need to encourage growth in faculty members [students] and the need to reward merit [assign grades]. (Page 1992, 15)

These statements suggest a close similarity of functions and of the tensions produced by those sometimes-conflicting functions. The dual roles the teacher is required to play with the student are the same as those the faculty colleague or administrator is required to perform with the faculty member being evaluated. There is the desire to encourage performance and promote growth. Our metaphors for this function include coach, colleague, collaborator, midwife, mentor, nurturer, questioner, listener, facilitator. There is also the need to evaluate that performance and growth, both as a part of the nurturing function and as a final decision-making act. Hence, the metaphors identified by Riegle and Rhodes of assessor, appraiser, rater, critic, and judge.

My preference, then, is simply for the overarching metaphor of the teacher. From this perspective, the departmental or campus macrocosm reflects the classroom microcosm, a teaching/learning environment in which the faculty or administrative evaluator functions like the classroom teacher. And the metaphorical perspective of the teacher alters one's attitude and approach:

> For evaluating faculty, like grading students, surely has other ends than culling and classifying and certifying. The linkages between evaluating and motivating—for faculty as for students—need to be continually explored. And the enhancement of a broad and humane learning for both faculty and students needs to be kept out there as that vital abstraction that justifies all this constant peering at each other. (Eble 1984, 100)

Some Promising Signs

As Barbara Page (1992) says, "Teaching is in the news" (15), and in a good way. Several recent initiatives have pointed toward a revised view of collegiate teaching and a greater incorporation of teaching into the reward and recognition systems of colleges and universities.

Some of these initiatives have been external ones, with various publics insisting on documentation of teaching effectiveness and learning effectiveness as an overall part of institutional effectiveness. But others have been internal, prompted, as Edgerton, Hutchings, and Quinlan (1991) note, "not only by presidents and trustees who want to reposition their campuses as teaching institutions, but by faculty who care deeply about teaching and sense a new legitimacy for their concerns in the emerging interest in undergraduate reform" (1).

Contributing also to this potential renaissance of teaching status are publications and projects such as Lynne Cheney's *Tyrannical Machines* (1990); Ernest Boyer's *Scholarship Reconsidered* (1990); the continuing impact of K. Patricia Cross and Thomas Angelo's classroom research initiatives, documented in *Classroom Assessment Techniques: A Handbook for Faculty* (1988); Arthur Chickering and Zelda Gamson's "Seven Principles for Good Practice in Undergraduate Education" (1987); Joseph Katz and Mildred Henry's *Turning Professors into Teachers: A New Approach to Faculty Development and Student Learning* (1988); Peter Seldin's *The Teaching Portfolio: A Practical Guide to Improved Performance and Promotion/Tenure Decisions* (1991); Russell Edgerton, Patricia Hutchings, and Kathleen Quinlan's *The Teaching Portfolio: Capturing the Scholarship in Teaching* (1991), the AAHE Teaching Initiative, begun in 1990; and Peter Seldin and Associates' *How Administrators Can Improve Teaching* (1990). In one way or another, all call for heightening the status of teaching and provide means toward that end.

Three of the most promising initiatives for the writing teacher are (1) an expanded definition of "scholarship," (2) the teaching portfolio as a means of "capturing the scholarship in teaching," and (3) discipline-specific classroom research on teaching and on the evaluation of teaching, represented by the essays in this collection.

Traditionally, in the triad of research, teaching, and service, the first has been recognized on most campuses as scholarship, the other two as something less. What is now being urged is a redefinition that would bring together the three activities as complementary manifestations of "scholarship" in a broader, overarching sense.

Such a new definition was proposed by Boyer in his *Scholarship Reconsidered* (1990), but it occurs earlier in *Building Communities: A Vision for a New Century* (1988), the report by the Commission on the Future of Community Colleges, which Boyer chaired:

> In addition to the scholarship of *discovering* knowledge, through research, it is also important to recognize the scholarship of *integrating* knowledge, through curriculum development, the scholarship of *applying* knowledge, through service, and, above all, the scholarship of *presenting* knowledge, through effective teaching. (26)

Such a redefinition would constitute radical change in many institutions. As Harriet Sheridan points out (1990), such change will not come easy:

> Substantial change in the social stratification of the academy to provide greater status to the teaching function of the profession will only come about from a combination of sustained national leverage, such as is now occurring, administrative energy directed toward this end in each institution, and faculty support within their disciplinary groups.... Only a sweeping review of the modes by which teaching is refereed, a review that is companion to the current national assessment movement but that is indigenous to the faculty of a campus, will lead to enhancement. (169, 174)

One such mode is the teaching portfolio. The subtitles of recent publications by Seldin (*A Practical Guide to Improved Performance and Promotion/Tenure Decisions;* 1991) and by Edgerton, Hutchings, and Quinlan (*Capturing the Scholarship in Teaching;* 1991) indicate their sense of its potential. In his preface, Seldin comments both on the need for and the capabilities of the portfolio:

> The quality of teaching has become a crucial concern at colleges and universities today. Swelling pressures from such diverse sources as the Carnegie Foundation for the Advancement of Teaching, the American Association for Higher Education, state legislatures, faculty and students have moved institutions to reconsider the importance of teaching and the role of the instructor in the classroom.
> Pivotal to this reconsideration is the issue of the reward system. In truth, it does little good to tout teaching excellence if faculty consistently perceive that only research is considered important. If outstanding teaching is to be encouraged, institutions must provide meaningful rewards to faculty for teaching.
> But how can professors document superior classroom performance or an outstanding effort to improve performance? The best way I know to provide such documentation is the teaching portfolio. Why? Because it documents both the complexity and individuality of good teaching. Today, the routine approach to evaluating teaching relies almost exclusively on student ratings. Portfolios go well beyond the routine approach. They include documents and materials from a number of important sources. Also, the routine approach to evaluation originates with and is controlled by administration. The portfolio concept, on the other hand, empowers faculty members to take charge of their own evaluations. (xi)

A third initiative, illustrated by this volume of essays, is discipline-based reflection and research on teaching-learning and the improvement of that teaching-learning in the writing classroom through more effective evaluation of teaching.

Indeed, if we are to take the initiative in this new climate of interest and emphasis in teaching, we will need an even better process for evaluating teaching than we have now. "The performance of each teacher in each classroom should ... be formally assessed," Ernest Boyer (1987) concludes, "if teaching is to assume the status it deserves" (155).

Such progress, both in raising the status and recognition of teaching and in effectively evaluating that teaching, should certainly please the many who, like Chaucer's Clerk, gladly learn and gladly teach.

Works Cited

Albert, Louis S. 1991. "Reclaiming the Public Trust." An Interview with Kay McClenney and Frank Newman of the Education Commission of the States. *AAHE Bulletin* 44(1): 3–8.

Aleamoni, Lawrence M., ed. 1987. *Techniques for Evaluating and Improving Instruction. New Directions for Teaching and Learning, no. 31.* San Francisco: Jossey-Bass.

Arreola, Raoul A. 1986. "Evaluating the Dimensions of Teaching." *Instructional Evaluation* 8: 4 –12.

Aubrecht, Judith. 1984. "Better Faculty Evaluation Systems." In Seldin, *Changing Practices*, 85–91.

Bleich, David. 1992. "Evaluation, Self-Evaluation, and Individualism." *ADE Bulletin* 101 (Spring): 9–14.

Boyer, Ernest L. 1987. *College: The Undergraduate Experience in America.* New York: Harper and Row.

———. 1990. *Scholarship Reconsidered: Priorities of the Professoriate.* Princeton, NJ: Carnegie Foundation for the Advancement of Teaching.

Braskamp, Larry A., Dale C. Brandenburg, and John C. Ory. 1984. *Evaluating Teaching Effectiveness: A Practical Guide.* Beverly Hills: Sage Publications.

Cashin, William E. 1990. "Assessing Teaching Effectiveness." In Peter Seldin and Associates, 89–103.

CCCC Committee on Teaching and Its Evaluation in Composition. 1982. "Evaluating Instruction in Writing: Approaches and Instruments." *College Composition and Communication* 33(2): 213–29.

Cheney, Lynne V. 1990. *Tyrannical Machines: A Report on Educational Practices Gone Wrong and Our Best Hopes for Setting Them Right.* Washington, D.C.: National Endowment for the Humanities.

Chickering, Arthur. 1984. "Faculty Evaluation: Problems and Solutions." In Seldin, *Changing Practices*, 91–96.

———, and Zelda Gamson. 1987. "Seven Principles for Good Practice in Undergraduate Education." *AAHE Bulletin* (March): 5 –10.

Commission on the Future of Community Colleges. 1988. *Building Communities: A Vision for a New Century.* Washington, D.C.: American Association of Community and Junior Colleges.

Cross, K. Patricia, and Thomas A. Angelo. 1988. *Classroom Assessment Techniques: A Handbook for Faculty.* Ann Arbor: National Center for Research on the Improvement of Postsecondary Teaching and Learning.

Davis, Barbara Gross, Michael Scriven, and Susan Thomas. 1987. *The Evaluation of Composition Instruction.* 2nd ed. New York: Teachers College Press.

Eble, Kenneth E. 1984. "New Directions in Faculty Evaluation." In Seldin, *Changing Practices,* 96–101.

Edgerton, Russell, Patricia Hutchings, and Kathleen Quinlan. 1991. *The Teaching Portfolio: Capturing the Scholarship in Teaching.* Washington, D.C.: American Association for Higher Education.

Elbow, Peter. 1986. *Embracing Contraries: Explorations in Learning and Teaching.* New York: Oxford University Press.

———. 1992. "Making Better Use of Student Evaluations of Teachers." *ADE Bulletin* 101 (Spring): 2–8.

Geis, George. 1984. The Context of Evaluation." In Seldin, *Changing Practices,* 101–8.

Katz, Joseph, and Mildred Henry. 1988. *Turning Professors into Teachers: A New Approach to Faculty Development and Student Learning.* New York: American Council on Education/Macmillan.

Larson, Richard L. 1970. *The Evaluation of Teaching College English.* New York: Modern Language Association of America.

Miller, Richard I. 1987. *Evaluating Faculty for Promotion and Tenure.* San Francisco: Jossey-Bass.

Page, Barbara. 1992. "Evaluating, Improving, and Rewarding Teaching: A Case for Collaboration." *ADE Bulletin* 101 (Spring): 15–18.

Riegle, Rodney P., and Dent M. Rhodes. 1986. "Avoiding Mixed Metaphors of Faculty Evaluation." *College Teaching,* 34(4): 123–28.

Seldin, Peter. 1984. *Changing Practices in Faculty Evaluation: A Critical Assessment and Recommendations for Improvement.* San Francisco: Jossey-Bass.

———. 1991. *The Teaching Portfolio: A Practical Guide to Improved Performance and Promotion/Tenure Decisions.* Bolton, MA: Anker.

———, and Associates. 1990. *How Administrators Can Improve Teaching: Moving from Talk to Action in Higher Education.* San Francisco: Jossey-Bass.

Sheridan, Harriet. 1990. "Ichabod Crane Dies Hard: Renewing Professional Commitments to Teaching." In Peter Seldin and Associates, 165–80.

Shulman, Lee. 1989. "Toward a Pedagogy of Substance." *AAHE Bulletin* 41(10): 8–13.

Southern Association of Colleges and Schools. 1991. *Criteria for Accreditation.* Decatur, GA: SACS.

II Evaluation Methods

4 The Devil Is in the Details: A Cautionary Tale

Edward M. White
California State University at San Bernardino

When Don came into my office, he was running his fingers nervously through his thinning hair. He piled some books and papers onto the corner of my desk and hurried back to shut the office door.

"What's the problem?" I asked.

"My students are filling in their teacher evaluation forms, and I feel terrible," he answered. "Can I really trust you?"

The question was as odd as his behavior. True, he was a School of Social Sciences part-timer in the writing-across-the-curriculum program I directed, but we had become friends over the years he had taught for the English department, and I knew he was a good teacher. I had observed his teaching several times before he had decided to switch to a school with less competition for writing classes. He used intelligent materials, gave good writing assignments, related well to students, worked hard at helping them revise papers, and was expert at using writing groups in his classes. When a part-time slot opened up in the School of Social Sciences, I had recommended him without reservation to teach their required upper-division writing course. He needed the money while he finished his second novel, and he was far better at teaching writing than any of the other part-timers (or full-timers, for that matter) in that school.

Don was, in short, perfectly typical of one large group of part-time teachers who perform much of the writing instruction in American colleges and universities: hard working, informed, serious about his teaching and his students, and, though underpaid, not at all interested in becoming a full-time faculty member. He was that logical contradiction, a permanent temporary part-timer, a position the Conference on College Composition and Communication said should be abolished, since, among other problems, it shares none of the academic freedom of the tenurable class. As WAC coordinator, my administrative job for teachers as good as Don was to take care of the bureaucratic machinery so they could do their job without distraction.

"You've always gotten good student evaluations before," I said cautiously. "Why should you be bothered now?"

"You just don't understand how these things are used in the social sciences," he replied with exasperation. "My neck's on the line, and I've been cheating. I can't live this way."

I was stunned. He sat down by my desk while his students were filling in the computer-readable evaluation form on his teaching and told me what was really going on with the part-timers.

Unlike the English department, which had voted to use faculty class visits and mentor conferences as an important part of the evaluation of part-timers, the School of Social Sciences used only the computer printouts summarizing the student evaluation forms. If your score fell below 3.0 out of a possible 4.0, you were fired. So the part-timers had worked out ways of manipulating the system, and some of the worst teachers were getting very high scores. The students knew that their ratings determined whether the teachers were kept on, so they used that knowledge to play their teachers for high grades.

"But you don't have to play that game," I said to Don. "You're a good enough teacher to get good ratings honestly."

Don shook his head. "Things have tightened up. There are six of us competing for four jobs next year. I can't play it straight anymore. The whole system makes me feel dirty."

Don had not gone very far down the scale of corruption. Before handing out the evaluation forms, he had returned a batch of student essays with what were, for him, fraudulent grades. He had simply given every paper either an A or A-, depending upon whether the student work was good or bad. He had then spent some time talking about his life as a single parent on a low income and telling how tough it was to work as a writer. He told the students how much he liked them personally and how much he was depending upon them, and then he came to my office.

He had not done what some others routinely did. He had not reduced the required work to half, and he did not promise everyone high grades. He would not consider going through the evaluation forms himself with an eraser, changing the ratings to make them better; he shuddered at the fellow who had confided that he filled in all the forms himself. But he still had done all he could manage to do to manipulate the system.

What was I to say to him, or to myself? After all, I had been, for years, one of the principal defenders of student ratings of faculty.

"You know, of course, that some research shows that the students won't let this kind of manipulation work."

"Sure," he said. "It may even be true for experimental conditions. But none of us believe it. Every part-timer cheats in one way or another."

We were, in fact, dealing with perceptions of student evaluations in our school, not with experimental data. As long as the part-timers *believed* that manipulation was necessary for high ratings, manipulation would occur. It did not matter if some experimental studies showed that hard graders can still receive high student ratings; the belief that easy grades and low demand lead to high ratings fed upon itself. As long as student evaluations were the only means of evaluating part-timers, and as long as the evaluation form was reduced to numbers, the corruption would continue.

I had served for some years on the university faculty evaluation committee and had steadily defended student evaluations ever since, despite the persistent problems of implementation. I had argued that the students were, in many cases, more honest and more dependable than were colleagues or department chair reports, at least in many departments. We had elected a series of ad hoc faculty committees to review and improve the rating form, and for two decades, those committees had been working hard and promising better and better results. The last committee had done intense statistical studies and had reformed the wording of the questions so that they clearly specified the student perceptions (not final judgments) that the ratings measured. All of us had studied the research and been convinced of the value of student perceptions of teaching. The students were always encouraged to write out comments as well as to check numerical boxes, and a few did make notes that, every once in a while, someone would bother to read.

But the devil is in the details. The fact was, virtually everyone involved in evaluating faculty, most particularly part-timers, felt themselves too busy to do more than to look at the reduction of student ratings to numbers. And when all we get is a number, the wording of the question does not make much difference. The English department was almost alone in visiting classes and in sending senior faculty to sit down with part-timers to find out what they were doing and why. And even the English department, faced with an increasing work load, was considering resorting to numerical reductions more and more.

Other problems had been evident to all of us on the university committee. For example, we could never figure out why the faculty in the School of Education, which was no better than most other schools of education, invariably received the highest student ratings; even the weakest of minds in that school received higher scores than the best minds in our distinguished School of Natural Sciences. Could that be a reflection of the much higher student grades in the education school? Of the low quality of textbooks in education, which made teachers look better? Of the large number of graduate students in education classes?

Of the simplicity of the material in comparison with the hard sciences? Or of the relative ease of teaching practice as compared with theory? Few of us knew what to believe, though everyone had a hypothesis. And no one believed the earnest protestations of the education representative, who asserted repeatedly that his school simply had the best teachers in the university.

Other injustices seemed less problematic, though still troubling. Most teachers with small classes did very well, particularly if the classes were performance oriented, such as physical education, counseling, or studio art, but nobody was able to do very well in a required course, particularly in writing or math. We supposed that students approached a required course with a different attitude than they brought to electives, and that attitude simply made it harder for the teacher to get high scores. Most of us felt that only truly extraordinary teachers can get high scores in large lecture classes, in which the teacher is a remote dot from the back rows. Classes with large numbers of one sex or of a particular racial group seemed to give higher scores to teachers of the same sex or race. Again and again, we noticed that comparisons of scores were unfair and misleading unless all the variables were controlled; yet the number of variables increased with every discussion. But everyone involved in evaluation made constant comparisons just the same. The controlled conditions of the research on student evaluations seemed never to apply in our world of real classes, real students, real jobs.

I had less trouble understanding why writing teachers, even the best of them, normally scored on the low side of student ratings. The logic seems clear enough: writing teachers are in the business of asking students to continue to improve work which the students feel is finished, of demanding more and better reading and writing than many students want to produce. Beginning writers want, and need, appreciation, rewards, and praise; good writing teachers will do much of that, but they will also offer criticism, demands for revision, and suggestions for improvement. We cannot expect many students to appreciate such hard demands, at least at the time. It is all too human for students to feel that a better teacher would be more appreciative of writing on which much labor has been expended.

The English department had tried to ameliorate that situation by refusing to allow the student ratings to be reduced to a single number or to play a dominant role in faculty evaluation. When we were a small department, we asked the senior faculty member who was evaluating a young teacher to serve as mentor as well as evaluator—to review a few sets of papers with comments on them, for instance, and to look over end-of-term student portfolios to notice improvement. The mentor's report weighed more heavily than the student ratings in the departmental recommendation. But as we turned from a small college into a large university, the part-timers were less and less comfortable with their mentors, and rumor had it that the time spent by the mentors was steadily decreasing. As funds grew smaller and the competition among departments for positions grew more fierce, the department had to defend its recommendations at the school level, and a part-timer (or even someone up for tenure) with low numbers was in trouble, whatever the department might say.

So we talked, Don and I, about the conflict between the theory of student evaluation and the practice. He brought up T. S. Eliot's argument about censorship, in his late, conservative essay, "Religion and Literature." All theory argues for censorship, Eliot had argued: literature affects people profoundly for good and for ill, and the corruption caused by corrupt literature can be severe. But Eliot then goes on to point out that, in practice, censorship always works badly: the wrong books are censored, for the wrong reasons, by the worst people. The conclusion is inescapable: theoretical arguments for censorship must give way before the practical results of censorship, which are always evil. The same logic, Don said, must apply to student evaluation of writing teachers: if the results in practice are so corrupting to teachers and to teaching, no theoretical argument is worth attending to.

After twenty minutes, Don morosely picked up his books and papers and returned to his class, where his students were waiting, their evaluations of him completed. I sat lost in thought. Surely there must be a way for student response to teaching to take forms beyond the reductionism of numbers; for student responses to be a part of teaching evaluation rather than the whole; for sensible, balanced, and responsible peer evaluation of teaching to consider student views of their teachers even at a large university. Small colleges manage it, I knew, though not easily. But I had to face the fact that my own school, dedicated for over two decades to student evaluation, had a system that had driven Don to say what he had said and to do what he had done.

I, of course, could not sit and think about this matter too long. My own writing class was about to meet and my students were to evaluate my own teaching. I began to get my materials together, thinking of the contrast between my own security as a tenured full professor and Don's insecurity. My job did not depend upon student evaluations, which I might choose to read or to ignore. Only the chair of the English department, an old friend, would see them, and he could be counted upon to say nothing, whatever they might indicate. Why, then, was I so nervous? I looked at the set of papers I had planned to return to the students at the start of class, and I thought about the low grades on many of them. Why look for trouble? I left the papers on my desk; I could give them out tomorrow, after the student evaluations had been turned in, just as well as today.

5 Peer Review of Writing Faculty

Ellen Strenski
University of California at Los Angeles

The principle of judgment by one's equals—peer review—has suffused common law since the *Magna Carta* in 1252. Today, confidence in academic peer review, confirmed by conventional wisdom about faculty governance, is enhanced by fashionable doctrines about the social construction of knowledge and the authority of group-sanctioned beliefs. The practice of academic peer review, a procedure for selecting publications as well as personnel, appears to promise, if not truth, then its closest approximation (Schlefer 1990, 5). The alternative may seem uninformed, capricious, or malevolent. As colleges and universities are increasingly held accountable for the quality of instruction, peer review assumes increasingly conspicuous importance as a source of data on which to base personnel decisions, and even as a mechanism for making those decisions.

Yet, in an unfavorable light, academic peer review may also seem inevitably conservative *peer advocacy*, not *peer review*, promoting sectarian—as opposed to wider institutional—interests, and impeding innovation. It can also imply institutional abdication of responsibility, which, so widely diffused, leaves no one to blame for incompetence. A major challenge for faculty review is to reconcile these perceptions which, in turn, shape and justify practice.

Meanwhile, the present practice of academic peer review is not monolithic. It continues to be shaped by legal pressures from court decisions, beginning earlier in this century with the AAUP codified doctrine of academic freedom, protected by tenure, to today's Supreme Court suits that allege discrimination, prohibited by Title VII legislation in the Civil Rights Act, and that urge disclosure of confidential peer-reviewed material.

The forms, questions, and guidelines presented in this chapter are a hybrid of many different sources; nonetheless, the author acknowledges the influence on them of Richard I. Miller's *Evaluating Faculty for Promotion and Tenure* (Jossey-Bass, 1987).

Academic peer review of writing instructors is further complicated by the somewhat mysterious nature of the activity—teaching writing—that is being reviewed. Evaluation is not like this everywhere. In the world beyond the ivy walls, managers—not peers—routinely evaluate employee job performance, using such categories as behavioral objectives and "goal setting" to examine employee productivity and performance. For example, a manager reviewing an employee's performance may typically say, "You must process ten percent more cash reports each fiscal month," according to an article on "Evaluating an Employee's Performance" (Buhler 1991, 17). Such human resource accounting, including employee evaluation, is a subject taught in M.B.A. programs. But this approach obviously won't do when student papers, not cash reports, are at issue. More appropriate to teaching, especially the teaching of writing, is peer review, a process derived from community recognition of the values that are implied in various class-related activities. That these standards are not easily stated as "goals," easily perceived and assessed by managers or administrators, does not make them less real, and peers are uniquely situated to make them materialize for scrutiny and appraisal.

Such peer review can range from simply gathering information about an instructor's teaching performance to be added to an instructor's dossier; to judging that information and information collected from other sources, e.g., student letters or course evaluations; to recommending, on the basis of this information, specific personnel decisions about the instructor's reappointment, promotion, or merit pay. As a source of information, peer review is a supplement or alternative to that provided by the instructor, by administrators, or by students. As a deliberative process, peer review enables instructors to participate, along with administrators, in employment decisions, thereby determining the nature of future faculty positions and assuming responsibility for them. Faculty, either undergoing or participating in peer review, and administrators endorsing the practice are wise to consider the implications of this undertaking. To provide such information and to suggest some guidelines for the process is the purpose of this chapter.

This chapter will deal exclusively with summative evaluation, that is, situations where an instructor's job security or professional advancement are at stake, depending on a judgment made about the quality of instruction and its consequent value to the institution. The other kind of evaluation, formative (see chapter 1 of this volume), wherein peers assess each other's teaching for the purpose of counseling and professional development, is a comparatively benign, unproblematic practice.

Indeed, lip service to the contrary, formative peer review—an excellent practice to help instructors improve their teaching—only works when it is distinguished as much as possible from summative evaluation (Nelson 1987, 85–86).

To date, peer review in the summative evaluation of teaching has been embodied in four practices: (1) confidential assessment by peers of a publication record; (2) classroom visits by peers to observe instructors; (3) classroom visits by peers to interview students; (4) peer committee review at the departmental level of a dossier and a subsequent committee recommendation to a dean. Each of these practices presents problems that can be anticipated and addressed. The major improvement in summative peer review, especially of writing instructors, would begin the whole process with the instructor's self-evaluation. This chapter will accordingly sketch these four kinds of current practice and their limitations, and then explain the vital contribution of self-evaluation to the process.

Confidential Assessment by Peers of a Publication Record

This is what most people mean by "academic peer review," a procedure modeled by the practice of research-university promotion and tenure committees who solicit confidential testimony from the instructor's colleagues at other institutions about the merit of the instructor's scholarship. As recently as 1990, in the *University of Pennsylvania v. EEOC*, the Supreme Court delivered a unanimous ruling that now calls into question the continuing confidentiality of such peer-reviewed materials. This means that now the EEOC can subpoena any peer-reviewed materials, even those of colleagues, for comparative purposes, when there is "reasonable cause" to suspect discrimination. "The ultimate consequence . . . is that many educational employment practices will be required to relinquish their veil of secrecy and be exposed to open scrutiny" (Robinson, Franklin, and Allen 1990, 369). According to "The Relationship between Access and Selectivity in Tenure Review Outcomes," a recent dissertation, "colleges with [a] confidential tenure process do not differ significantly in participation or results of process from colleges with [an] open tenure process" (qtd. in Frost 1991, 349). So disclosure may not be such a bad thing, in spite of arguments about its alleged chilling effect on reviewers who would not then provide forthright testimony. In any case, any peer review of a publication record, that is, of material which formerly was protected by a blanket appeal to an institution's academic freedom, may now be liable to public scrutiny if discrimination is charged. The clear implication is that the criteria used for such peer review must be job-related and defensible. For example, one legal analysis of *University of Pennsylvania v. EEOC* suggests that if collegiality, for instance, is an important aspect of faculty quality, then that criterion should be spelled out and included specifically with the other, more traditional criteria about scholarship, service, and so on (Robinson, Franklin, and Allen 1990, 369).

These now potentially public criteria are one thing; the "publication record" of a writing instructor is another. Composition instructors are often not tenurable. Their value is usually their teaching performance, not the "research" found in typical "P and T" dossiers. Is there, then, any counterpart at all of such documents which can be scrutinized by peers? Is there a written trace of classroom performance and teaching effectiveness? Yes, indeed. Consider the ephemera produced for and by any composition class: dittoed and photocopied handouts, syllabi, sample papers, assignment sheets, editing guides, graded and commented upon papers, thank-you notes from students. These can, and ought, to be collected into a tangible record, a "teaching portfolio," glossed and thereby contextualized with the instructor's explanations (Watkins 1990, A15–A17; Seldin 1991; Edgerton, Hutchings, and Quinlan 1991).

A teaching portfolio, however, is not only a logistical convenience which collects documentary evidence of teaching effectiveness for scrutiny by an instructor's peers; it is also a gauge of the instructor's writing skill, which, along with classroom teaching performance, surely is also a major job qualification for a writing instructor. The ability to write clearly and forcefully is valued by hiring committees who screen letters of application and who often request syllabi and writing samples from candidates. No one would be hired to teach writing who had a wooden ear, oblivious to the sound and shape of prose, or who was unable to organize and sequence thoughts on the page. So, too, no one would hire an applicant to teach studio art who couldn't draw; to teach music, who couldn't play or sing; or architecture, who had never designed and built. If writing ability counts at the hiring stage, so should it, too, for retention and promotion. Not many writing instructors publish: poems, stories, technical reports, journal articles, etc. But all do prepare classroom materials which, along with any publications, can constitute a teaching portfolio, that is, the equivalent of a publication record.

Just how this criterion of writing ability, illustrated in the teaching portfolio and possibly elsewhere, is weighted along with other criteria, which are, for instance, evidenced in student evaluations or student improvement, should be discussed and established before the review. Two issues are at stake in this discussion: appropriateness and equivalency. Consider, for example, the writing skill of two instructors who both teach freshman composition. One is a prolific writer of poems, most unpublished; the other moonlights as an editor helping foreign-born engineers revise their technical reports. The poems and edited reports are both evidence of writing ability, both are related somewhat to classroom instruction, and both can therefore be included in a teaching portfolio along with the more conventional material (syllabi, assignments, etc.). But how can they be compared and, if necessary, ranked? The answer must involve acknowledging the mission of writing instruction and the corresponding teaching duties at the particular institution (e.g., perceived as service to other campus departments or as a belletristic complement to a traditional English curriculum), and, indeed, the wider mission of the institution (e.g., a liberal arts or technical college). Candidates for review should anticipate this problem and, in their initial self-evaluation, offer a compelling justification and context for their peers' scrutiny of this material. Peers should make their criteria for judging writing ability as specific to the courses taught as possible. A point of departure is illustrated in figure 1, a form from UCLA's Office of Instructional Development. This form and the others in this chapter are compilations put together over the years by that office. Particularly useful here as a tool to guide peer reviewers is the column "Suggested Focus in Examining Dossier Materials." As with all such forms, this one would have to be modified to fit the expectations demanded of writing faculty at institutions other than research universities where, for instance, mentoring graduate student assistants would not be applicable.

In passing it is worth noting that item #4 gets at something that, when tailored to writing instruction, can elicit very important information about the job performance of writing instructors at all institutions, which peers are in a particularly privileged position to acknowledge and judge. This function is advising, both personal and academic. Richard Miller (1987) reports ten "Criteria for Evaluating Faculty Performance by Major Input Groups," these input groups being department chair, colleagues, dean, and students, and the ten criteria ranging from scholarship, to teaching, to professional growth (111). Miller points out dramatically that, although the other input groups did not particularly care about it, students weighted advising higher than anything else (weighted 70), higher even than teaching (weighted 60). Prized above all else by students, advising is an institutional function, certainly related to teaching and job performance, that writing faculty can perform better than almost any of their colleagues who teach other subjects. Why? Because the small classes and intimate contact with students over their drafts—the drafts often being about personal be-

COLLEAGUE EVALUATION
Teaching Materials and Procedures Appraisal

Question	Dossier Materials	Suggested Focus in Examining Dossier Materials
1. What is the quality of materials used in teaching?	Course outline Syllabus Reading list Text used Study guide Media Handouts Problem sets Assignments	Are these materials current? Do they represent the best work in the field? Are they adequate and appropriate to course goals? Do they represent superficial or thorough coverage of course content?

Peer Reviewer's Rating: Low _____ Very High
Comments:

2. What kind of intellectual tasks were set by the teacher for the students (or did the teacher succeed in getting students to set them for themselves), and howdid the students perform?	Copies of graded exams. Examples of graded research papers. Examples of teacher's feedback to students on written work. Grade distribution. Descriptions of student performance, e.g., class presentation, etc. Examples of completed assignments.	What was the level of intellectual performance achieved by the students? What kind of work was given an A? a B? a C? Did the students learn the department curriculum expected for this course? How adequately do the tests or assignments represent the kinds of student performance specified in the course objectives?

Peer Reviewer's Rating: Low _____ Very High
Comments:

Fig. 1. Examples of evaluation criteria used in a peer review of a teaching portfolio.

| 3. How knowledge-able is this faculty member in the subjects taught? | Evidence in teaching materials. Record of atten-dance at regional or national meetings. | Has the instructor kept in thoughtful contact with developments in his or her field? Is there evidence of acquaintance with ideas and findings of other scholars? (This question addresses the scholarship necessary to good teaching. It is *not* concerned with scholarly research publication.) |

Peer Reviewer's Rating: Low _____ Very High
Comments:

| 4. Has this faculty member assumed responsibilities related to the department's or the university's teaching mission? | Record of service on department curri-culum committee, honors program, advising board of teaching support service, special committees (e.g., to examine grading policies, admission standards, etc.). Description of activities in supervising graduate students learning to teach. Evidence of design of new courses. | Has he or she become a departmental college citizen in regard to teaching responsibilities? Does this faculty member recognize problems that hinder good teaching, and does he or she take a responsible part in trying to solve them? Is the involvement of the faculty member appropriate to his or her academic level (e.g. assistant professors may sometimes become over involved to the detriment of their scholarly and teaching activites)? |

Peer Reviewer's Rating: Low _____ Very High
Comments:

Fig. 1. *Continued.*

5. To what extent is this faculty member trying to achieve excellence in teaching?	Factual statement of what activities that faculty member has engaged in to improve his or her teaching. Examples of questionnaires used for formative purposes. Examples of changes made on the basis of feedback.	Has he or she sought feedback about teaching quality, explored alternative teaching methods, made changes to increase student learning? Has he or she sought aid in trying new teaching ideas? Has he or she developed special teaching materials or participated in cooperative efforts aimed at upgrading teaching quality?

Peer Reviewer's Rating: Low_____ Very High
Comments:

Fig. 1. *Continued.*

liefs—give writing faculty a unique opportunity to influence students. Moreover, the readings on which writing assignments are based are increasingly interdisciplinary and multicultural. In writing classes, students are in a unique position to integrate knowledge and to demonstrate that ability. Just how this service can be documented in the teaching portfolio, beyond assignments and commented-upon drafts of papers, is another issue, but peers, often jammed into small offices which they share with each other, are in the best position to observe at least the amount, if not the quality, of conferencing that goes on between instructor and students, and they can appreciate the nature and intended effects of the questioning prompts written on students' drafts and papers.

In any case, a teaching portfolio for a writing instructor does double duty: it documents and presents classroom materials as a measure of instruction, as does any teaching portfolio, but in addition, it illustrates the important, job-specific qualification of writing ability. Peers who judge the portfolio can do so with relative confidence (that is, relative to their colleagues in other academic disciplines) because whatever else they are, writing instructors are expert readers of texts and are therefore especially well qualified to examine and appraise this documentary evidence.

Classroom Visits

To find out how well an instructor is performing in the classroom, the obvious solution seems to be to go and take a look. And who better to send but another instructor? However, it's not so simple. The literature on evaluation warns about the accuracy and usefulness of information obtained through classroom observation unless it involves multiple observers who are specially trained and who return to the classroom several times (Centra 1975, 334–336). The predictable problems (e.g., the observer's presence skewing the class atmosphere and therefore student and instructor behavior) are exacerbated in writing classes, which tend to be smaller than the typical class and less dependent on a lecture format. Not only that, but students often spend time in a writing class writing, which is about as exciting to watch as corn growing. Nonetheless, the instructor's behavior during intervals when students are writing (for example, circulating to give assistance or reading a novel) is worth noting.

Classroom observation has two advantages: one magical and rhetorical, the other, logistical. In my experience, a classroom visit corroborates the accuracy of assessment derived from other sources. Its absence is troublesome to those who must act on an evaluation report. Since its usefulness as a source of evidence is disputed, a class visit assumes, then, a ceremonial function in the review process, which ought not to be disparaged so much as exploited for rhetorical effect. This inclusion is especially important for any fledgling peer-review process which must argue not only directly for its assessment of instructors, but also, indirectly, for its continuing right to exist.

The second advantage of classroom observation is logistical and derives from the standard practice of using checklists (Miller 1987). The value of checklists themselves is questionable, especially when items are given a numerical weight. For example, thirteen years later, I am still puzzled (and slightly angry) about a report of a class visit that gave me a "4" (above average) in answer to the checklist question "Was the instructor sensitive to student responses?" but a "5" (excellent) to the next checklist question "Did the general class atmosphere reflect mutual respect and regard?" Instructor sensitivity and classroom atmosphere are important features of instruction, but a numerical scale is too gross an instrument for capturing fine distinctions, quite apart from the observer's ability to perceive them in the first place. The administrative impulse to quantify performance, like the manager, cited earlier, who counted cash reports processed each fiscal month, is understandable, particularly when instructors are competing for reappointment or advancement and when administrators want comparable data for ranking purposes. But the impulse to reduce classroom observation to numbers must be resisted. Moreover, the generic classroom observation checklists do not easily fit writing classes, which are typically smaller and conducted as workshops, not lectures.

Nonetheless, the checklists have heuristic power. They can serve as a point of departure to focus discussion between the instructor and the peer observer(s) on the checklist categories, such as instructor sensitivity and classroom atmosphere. By doing so, they can generate more accurate, course-specific, and therefore fair and useful observation, even if the resulting information is less easily manipulated than numbers. For example, the form from UCLA reproduced in figure 2 includes ques- tions that can't be answered "Yes," or "No," or "Somewhat"—the verbal equivalents of numbers. They place some responsibility on the observer(s) for a kind of ethnographic reporting and interpretation. For example, rather than the flatfooted question "Did students seem interested and participate?" the form asks "Describe the form and extent of student interest and participation." And even this all-purpose form, geared to typical UCLA lecture classes, needs to be tailored to the writing class being observed. For example, if peer editing of drafts is on the classroom agenda, a checklist item might solicit information about students' readiness and willingness to work together—how quickly and enthusiastically they undertake the task. Or, as another example, if the lesson includes a worksheet or handout exercise on stylistic analysis, the observer can look for students' ease in making connections with their own drafts.

Such changes on the checklist can be made in the preliminary meeting. Note the instructions on this form. A preliminary meeting is essential to contextualize the observation. Moreover, common courtesy and professional collegiality demand such a meeting of minds before the observation. The instructor and the peer reviewer(s) should agree on a time to visit and on what will happen, both in the particular class and in the observation, and how the results of the observation will be reported and used; for example, whether they will be placed in the teaching portfolio or filed with other confidential data.

Classroom Interviews

Closely related to peer classroom observation but—to judge from practice as reported by UCLA's Office of Instructional Development—much

COLLEAGUE EVALUATION
Classroom Observation Report

Instructor: _____ Course: _____

Number of students present: _____ Date: _____

Evaluator(s): _____

INSTRUCTIONS: Several days prior to the classroom observation, the instructor should provide the evaluator(s) with a copy of the course syllabus containing course objectives, content, and organization. The instructor should explain to the evaluator(s) the instructional goals and the means by which the goals for the class will be accomplished.

Within three days after the visit, the evaluator(s) should meet with the instructor to discuss observations and conclusions.

Please use the reverse side of this page to elaborate on your comments.

1. Describe the lesson taught, including the subject, objectives, and methods of instruction used.

2. Describe the instructor's teaching as it relates to content mastery, breadth, and depth.

3. How well organized was the lecture; or more specifically, how well organized was the introductory portion, the body of the lecture, and the conclusion of the lecture?

4. How clear was the presentation, e.g., defines new terms, uses clear and relevant examples, etc.?

5. Describe the instructor's presentation style, e.g., voice characteristics, speaking style, nonverbal communication, and whether or not it was satisfactory.

6. Do you consider the instruction to be of an appropriate or inappropriate level and quality? How suitable is this material for the class?

7. Does the instructor establish and maintain contact with the students?

8. Describe the form and extent of student interest and participation.

9. Did the instructor encourage critical thinking and analysis?

10. Did the instructor demonstrate enthusiasm for the subject matter?

11. What are the instructor's major strengths? Weaknesses?

12. What specific recommendations would you make to improve the instructor's teaching in this class?

13. Do you believe your visitation was at a time when you were able to fairly judge the nature and tenor of the teaching-learning process?

Fig. 2. Example of evaluation criteria used in a peer review based on classroom observation.

less frequently performed are peer classroom interviews of students. In this procedure, one or two peers come to the class for the last fifteen or twenty minutes; they are introduced by the instructor, who then leaves the classroom; and then they interview the students. The purpose is to gather information that is richer than that received from student comments on standardized end-of-term questionnaires. Peer instructors can focus the interview on writing-specific activities, e.g., how drafts of papers are revised, and they can follow up on responses. UCLA provides instructors with three general guidelines for such interviews:

1. Begin the interview with overview questions to relax the students. Examples are questions like the following: What's your major? Why are you taking this course? (required? elective?)

2. Ask general questions followed by more specific ones for clarity or depth. Examples include items similar to the following: What methods of instruction do you prefer? Is there anything that interferes with your learning in this class?

3. Avoid leading questions which may result in extreme or nonrepresentative answers related to the situation. A contrasting example follows:

   Avoid: Do you think the tests are too hard?

   Better: What is your general impression of the tests?

As with classroom observation, classroom interviews can be structured with a checklist form. The one reproduced in figure 3, another from UCLA, like all such forms, should be modified to fit a writing class. For example, question #5 about lectures would usually be inappropriate and should therefore be omitted. However, it does provide another model for emulation or modification. The instructions here are important, especially the need to reassure the class that individual students will not be identified and that therefore they will be protected from any retribution if they speak forthrightly. Such a classroom interview provides a fuller measure of student opinion than does the use of a ques-tionnaire alone. However, like the student questionnaires discussed in chapter 8 of this volume, classroom interviews, as measures of teaching, are limited, and student opinion, however derived, must always be carefully contextualized.

In addition to the immediate purpose of providing textured information for summative evaluation, these peer interviews have another public relations benefit. They impress students with the institution's willingness to monitor the quality of instruction and to attend to consumer satisfaction. Standardized end-of-term questionnaires, of course,

---

STUDENT INTERVIEWS

Student Interview Schedule

Instructor: _____ Course: _____

Number of students present: _____ Date: _____

Consultant(s): _____

INSTRUCTIONS: Explain the voluntary and confidential nature of the interview, and that individual students will not be identified. Stress that all opinions are welcome. Have either individual students or groups of students address the following questions:

1. What do you like about the course?

2. What do you think needs improvement?

3. What suggestions have you for bringing about these improvements?

4. Did you learn something that you considered to be valuable and interesting?

5. Does the instructor demonstrate enthusiasm for the subject matter?

6. How well organized are the lectures?

7. How effectively does the instructor interact with the students?

8. Does the instructor cover an adequate breadth of the materials?

9. Are you satisfied with the examination/grading process? Do you receive adequate feedback on all assignments and examinations?

Fig. 3. Examples of evaluation criteria used in a peer review based on student interviews.

are intended to accomplish the same result, but the personal participation in the process by one or two peer faculty enhances its seriousness. In any case, students respond positively to such peer classroom interviews.

Peer Review by Committee

The three previously described practices (peer review of a publication record, peer visits to classrooms, and peer interviews of students) can be conducted by individuals who then generate information to be added to a dossier or teaching portfolio. The dossier itself is then judged by someone else (e.g., program administrators, a department chair, a dean, a college committee on academic personnel) who decides about the instructor's employment future.

However, another arrangement is to involve not just individual peers from whom information is solicited, but a committee of peers. Contrasted with outsiders, these peers may have a more immediate investment in maintaining quality instruction. Such a peer committee can undertake more or less responsibility, acting either as a simple clearinghouse for material (packaging, advancing, and presenting the teaching portfolio and other checklist forms or reports to the appropriate decision maker) or as an adjudicating body itself (not just assembling, but also judging the evidence and making recommendations based on it).

Two operating pressures shape the practice of any peer-review committee that has any real influence. One is the internal threat of competition. The other is the external opportunity for marketing, given that the committee reports are read beyond the writing program and directly reflect on the program's quality. Both pressures work toward peer advocacy, not peer judgment, if by judgment is meant the possibility of a negative verdict, that is, an instructor being judged not adequate to the demands of the institution. And both encourage exaggeration in final evaluation reports since the only way to damn a colleague often seems to be with faint praise. Real praise then becomes hyperbole.

Since few writing instructors enjoy the protected objectivity of tenure, those serving on a peer-review committee are often in competition with the instructor(s) being reviewed, if not immediately then at least somewhere down the line. How can the inhibiting threat of competition or retaliation be minimized so that committee reports are produced that are not damaged and discredited to start with by rhetorical inflation? How to get institutionally useful information from peer-review committee reports?

Anonymity for peer reviewers is not only suspect, given potential legal pressures for disclosure, but is logistically impossible. As one UCLA Writing Programs lecturer conceded, "I can't sit in on so-and-so's class with a paper bag over my head." Better are structural arrangements to safeguard the integrity of the process, and a process that is publicly endorsed to start with. The example of UCLA Writing Programs may be instructive. Its approximately forty full-time, nontenurable lecturers are reappointed annually up to six years, at which point they undergo a major review and are offered a subsequent three-year appointment if judged to be "excellent." Yearlong discussion involving all faculty and administrators in the program resulted in the following peer-review policy.

A faculty advisory committee began the process by giving the director a list of names of possible peer-review committee members. The director selected four lecturers from this list and appointed them as a personnel committee. Once appointed, this committee elected a chair. Two members continued on the committee the following year; one of these continuing members serves as chair, the director again appointing the two remaining committee members.

After individual consultation with candidates for the major review, the personnel committee appoints members and chairs of ad hoc committees. A separate ad hoc committee of three lecturers is appointed for each candidate. Personnel committee members instruct ad hoc committees in proper procedures, review ad hoc committee reports, and produce final copies of these reports, which are submitted to the director. Such a diffused but coordinated arrangement has worked well so far to ensure that neither enemies nor cronies of an instructor can pack an ad hoc committee and thereby unfairly influence the outcome. The personnel committee, with its oversight function and comparative perspective, helps ensure that ad hoc committee reports are adequate and consistent.

All of this adds up to a lot of time and effort. However, it all has been assumed with good will, and thus far the process is working better than any alternative. A side benefit is professional development all around, as peer reviewers learn about and come to appreciate other ways of doing things.

The Need to Begin Peer Review with Self-Evaluation

It seems only fair to begin the review process of any instructor with that instructor's self-evaluation, or, more precisely, self-presentation. This beginning is a letter of application from the instructor which frames the instructor's teaching record, embodied in the teaching portfolio, and which makes a case for reappointment, promotion, or merit pay. This opportunity is even more essential for a writing instructor. Granted, every discipline has different pedagogical approaches. For example, some historians believe their approach of presenting students with facsimile primary documents in a case study of, say, the Civil War, is the best way to develop students' ability to sift and assess evidence, and thereby learn to think historically. Other historians believe the best way is to engage students in the study of problems, e.g., racism, and teach them to probe for causes. Nonetheless, contrasted with other disciplines, writing pedagogy seems especially fragmented.

Consider the variety of pedagogical beliefs informing the multiplicity of textbooks displayed at a Conference on College Composition and Communication convention—everything from literature-based style curricula through peer workshop/personal writing to cross-curricular service courses. Beliefs about the best way to teach writing are held passionately. How, then, can peers evaluate each other when they may hold radically different pedagogical beliefs? How can one instructor who conducts peer workshops on personal and group writing, who treasures the "personal voice" and assigns autobiography and journals, review a colleague who assigns research papers related to student majors, e.g., on insurance companies, and who, in the eyes of the first instructor, has sold out to the economics department and other departments on campus?

Several resources address this problem. One, already mentioned, is to distribute responsibility among a peer group of reviewers, as illustrated by UCLA Writing Programs, but this only works if the program is large enough. A second is the instructor's initial self-presentation, which makes the case for his or her pedagogical practice and in the process establishes the terms within which this practice should be reviewed. The third is research by Edward M. White (1989), which identifies six basic approaches to writing instruction, thereby providing a comparative context for appreciating the values of each approach.

It is the writing instructor's opportunity and challenge, but it is also his or her responsibility, to begin the review process by making the best case possible for reappointment, promotion, or whatever. If a writing instructor cannot write such a letter, either because he or she is not aware of, and therefore can't explain and justify, pedagogical principles, or because he or she lacks adequate powers of written expression, then the instructor should not be reappointed or promoted. With such a letter, however, the peer-review process can proceed on the terms established in it.

Particularly useful for establishing these terms is the taxonomy of writing instruction generated by Edward M. White's (1989) study of 418 California State University writing instructors (38–55). What White found were six "patterns" or "approaches" to instruction: literature, peer workshop, individualized writing lab, text-based rhetoric, basic skills, and service course. White found them at all levels, from remedial to advanced, and at all faculty ranks. Each approach has its own particular strengths and weaknesses. None is best. However, as White maintains, "We can reasonably expect writing teachers to know what they are doing in the writing class, and why" (55). Hence, the challenge and legitimacy of beginning a review process with a statement from the instructor, especially if peers are involved, peers who may champion very different approaches in their own classes. White's research is an especially helpful aid for any writing instructor contemplating the principles governing his or her practice and facing the task of articulating and defending them for a personnel review.

Conclusion

Peer review of writing instructors is a matter of generating documents: the teaching portfolio or dossier to be scrutinized, checklist reports of class observations and visits, perhaps a peer committee report assessing the instructor being reviewed or a report that makes recommendations based on that assessment. Peer review is also a matter of procedure: selecting the peer reviewer(s), determining the peer reviewer's tasks and authority, safeguarding the process. The best policy is to make peer review as open as possible: to establish a policy arrived at by consensus so that everyone knows what is happening to whom, by whom, and when.

Peer review of writing faculty *is* a good idea. Although universally feared, it has benefits. Formative peer review results in improved teaching. Summative peer review results in responsible accounting and also publicity for very real personal and programmatic achievements. Writing faculty, compared to other faculty, are particularly well qualified for this task of peer review. Writing faculty peers are skilled readers of texts, such as an instructor's self-evaluation or teaching portfolio. And they, as well as the instructor(s) being reviewed, are skilled writers; they can be expected to write effective evaluation reports. Although in no way foolproof, peer review is an important source of useful information and judgment. Its problems can be anticipated, addressed, and minimized if care is taken all around by instructors being reviewed, by peers, and by administrators who endorse, initiate, guide, and protect the process.

Works Cited

Buhler, Patricia. 1991. "Evaluating an Employee's Performance." *Supervision: The Magazine of Industrial Relations and Operating Management* 52: 17–19.

Centra, John A. 1975. "Colleagues as Raters of Classroom Instruction." *Journal of Higher Education* 46: 327–37.

Edgerton, Russell, Patricia Hutchings, and Kathleen Quinlan. 1991. *The Teaching Portfolio: Capturing the Scholarship in Teaching*. Washington, D.C.: American Association for Higher Education.

Frost, Lynda E. 1991. Shifting Meanings of Academic Freedom: An Analysis of University of Pennsylvania v. EEOC." *Journal of College and University Law* 17: 329–50.

Miller, Richard I. 1987. *Evaluating Faculty for Promotion and Tenure.* San Francisco: Jossey-Bass.

Nelson, Marylin J. 1987. "Peer Review in the English Classroom." *English Journal* 76(1): 85–86.

Robinson, Robert. K., Geralyn McClure Franklin, and Billie Morgan Allen. 1990. "University of Pennsylvania v. EEOC: The Demise of Academic Privilege in the Peer-Review Process." *Labor Law Journal* 41: 364–69.

Schlefer, Jonathan. 1990. "Truth, Beauty, and Peer Review." *Technology Review* 93: 5.

Seldin, Peter. 1991.*The Teaching Portfolio: A Practical Guide to Improved Performance and Promotion/Tenure Decisions.* Bolton, MA: Anker.

Watkins, Beverly T. 1990. "New Technique Tested to Evaluate College Teaching: Effort Uses Portfolios to Document Professors' In-class Performance." *Chronicle of Higher Education,* May 16: A15–A17.

White, Edward M. 1989. *Developing Successful College Writing Programs.* San Francisco: Jossey-Bass.

6 The Observer Observed: Retelling Tales In and Out of School

Anne Marie Flanagan
Temple University

Few people question the need for classroom observations. They take place every day and will continue to take place as long as there are teachers and students. But although the classroom observation is an enshrined educational practice, neither the art of observation nor the conditions under which observations take place have been adequately examined or perfected. Moreover, the very purpose of the classroom observation is continually debated, producing a prevailing sense of confusion among those who are observed and those who are charged with observing. Is the classroom observation to be supportive, an act of collaboration between observer and observed, or is it to be a tool of evaluation? Is it, and must it necessarily be, both collaborative and evaluative? If the observation is to accomplish both of these contradictory ends, how are the ground rules of the observation established to accommodate such contradictions?

Despite the best intentions to produce a collaborative observation situation, the charge to evaluate must fall to someone. Evaluation is necessary. Good teachers must be rewarded for their efforts and be encouraged to continue working hard and striving to be better. Poor teachers need to improve their performance if they wish to continue teaching. They need help and guidance to develop their skills. But all those involved in the work of evaluating teachers must be aware of the forces operating within their own particular contexts. Issues of authority and power must be taken into consideration and treated openly. Differences in rank, gender, class, and race and the peculiar concerns of the teaching assistant must be addressed. Above all, those responsible for training teachers must have clearly defined objectives concerning the evaluation of teachers. Those involved in this important endeavor must

I am indebted to Marge Murray for sharing her keen interest in observation practices with me; to Liz Hodges for her "ethnographic" model of classroom observation; and to Susan Wells for her valuable insights into the politics of the observation.

not find themselves at cross purposes, speaking languages that engender confusion, uncertainty, and sometimes opposition.

It is not surprising that such confusion exists. What is surprising is that little is done to explore the reasons for this confusion. There is a need to approach each observation as a critical act and to acknowledge both the forces at work in the observation and the ways in which the observer is implicated in the process (Brodkey 1987, 30, 47). As a recent participant in a meta-ethnography of a basic writing program, I was in a unique position to analyze some of the forces which make observations such problematic adventures. I was able to look at observations from both inside and outside, since I was charged with observing observers. I studied the process by which an observer negotiated her way through a maze of directives about observations in a deft dance through the cross purposes of the observation. Following this observer, two things became apparent. First, she was caught in an extremely complex observational environment, and second, her position as a senior teaching assistant acting as observer was ill-defined in regard to power and authority. What could she say? What might she want to say to a peer? What was she obliged to say to her superior? What did she want to say to her superior? Although these questions arise more frequently when power is distributed asymmetrically, as in the case of the teaching assistant observer, such questions arise routinely in every observation context, and an effort must be made to answer them.

All observation contexts are murky. I would like to open a window into the politics of a particularly opaque observation context. To begin with, it is necessary to recognize that the rules and customs governing observations do not necessarily evolve in an orderly pattern over time. Often, observation methods are simply entrenched in an institution and are followed long after their usefulness has been exhausted. Or, observations are carried on in a highly idiosyncratic manner, reflecting the tastes and biases of an individual who happens to be "in charge" of observations in a given academic year. Many times, those who supervise observations and observers fail to take into account the dynamics of power, class, gender, and race between observer and observed. What happens, for example, when a female teacher is observed by a male or when a female observes a male teacher? In a study that I conducted a few years ago, the findings of which were presented at the Penn State Conference on Rhetoric and Composition, I found that very interesting things indeed were happening. Female observers were more likely to describe a male teacher's performance as being "in control" and his grasp of material as "excellent." Mention was made of a male teacher's "solid intellectual understanding of what to teach" and that another male teacher was "strong in the theoretical aspects of teaching." Conversely, when female teachers were evaluated by either male or female observers, there were no references to female teachers' intellect or to their handling of abstract or theoretical concepts. Female observers reported that their female teaching counterparts were not "in control." One female observer described a female teacher's performance in this way: "Students were talking to each other . . . for quite some time the teacher seemed to be completely out of the discussion." (This statement in another context, perhaps in the hands of a male observer commenting on the performance of a male teacher, might be interpreted as a masterful transference of authority from teacher to students, empowering students to carry on their own discussion.) In another case, a male observer described a female teacher as exercising "too much control . . . teacher needs a more open view." No such negative remarks, either by male or female observers, were made about male teachers exercising control in their classrooms. The purpose of this chapter is not to report in detail the findings of my previous study, but to suggest that observations must be seen not as isolated moments in human relations, but as microcosms of the academic communities in which they take place.

The observation on which I wish to concentrate was complicated by confusion over the purpose of the observation and by the weak position of the teaching assistant observer. Unlike the scenario where observation methods have become entrenched to the point of petrification, the atmosphere at my institution was lively and in flux. The observer whom I followed entered an environment where much thought had been given to developing effective methods of observation. A spirited dialogue was already in progress. For the past three or four years, my university had been engaged in rethinking its standards or guidelines for observations. A quantitative scale for rating classroom performance had been proposed and rejected; various observation rubrics had been in circulation, themselves the cumulative effort of many voices ranging from former directors of the basic writing program, to faculty supervisors, to teaching assistants who had served as mentors. Finally, added to this collection of voices were those of two new administrators with their own notions of how to shape observations.

The dialogue turned from developing a methodology of observation to considering the exact purpose of the classroom observation. The question being debated now was whether a classroom observation could help a teacher improve her performance without being evaluative or judgmental. Observers were told to view observations as "collaborative efforts." There was to be no mention of "good" or "poor" teaching. In fact, observers were instructed to talk with teachers about their "observations," not their "conclusions" or "evaluations." At the same time, however, observers wanted to know what to look for when visiting classrooms. Therefore, a set of criteria was introduced to aid observers in focusing their attention. These criteria dealt with questions of organization, sequencing of classroom activities, student and teacher interaction, questioning strategies, etc. So despite the best intentions to reform and clarify the purpose and methods of observation, what resulted in this observation context was confusion and two separate languages, one that resisted evaluation and one that called out for it. What I want to uncover and reveal are the ways in which the observer negotiated her way between these two opposing languages. By documenting the observer's difficult path through the observation, it is possible to see the degree to which conflicting opinions about the purpose of the observation make the observer's job extremely difficult and reduce her effectiveness as an observer.

I find Mikhail Bakhtin's (1981) notion of "authoritative" discourse to be especially valuable as a methodological or critical tool for following the observer's progress or lack thereof. I believe, as Bakhtin does, that the social context, "the authentic environment of an utterance, the environment in which it lives and takes shape," is of the utmost importance (272). In the context of the observation, someone is ultimately in charge—someone's words carry the weight of authority. In this case, the voices of those directing the writing programs carry with them the "authoritativeness of tradition, of generally acknowledged truths, of the official line and other similar authorities." Bakhtin says that this is authoritative discourse and that it cannot be represented, only transmitted (344). The tradition of authority is powerful; however, no matter how authoritative this discourse is, it holds within itself the seeds of its own destruction or transformation. When authoritative discourse is transmitted, it is ever so slightly tinged or infected with another's speech and is on its way to being represented rather than transmitted. The teaching assistant observer finds it extremely difficult to oppose these voices of authority, but she finds ways to resist them and to negotiate her way between the language of collaboration and the language of evaluation that are expressed by the authoritative voices of her superiors.

My knowledge of the observer's experiences was gained through interviews. During these interviews an informal narrative style developed. I did not ask scripted questions or insist upon any particular format for the interview. Because she proceeded by means of a narrative, the observer was able to tell a story about her observation experiences. Again, Bakhtin provides a useful frame for understanding not only what the observer had to say about observing, but also how she chose to tell the story. The observer employed what Bakhtin calls the "two basic modes recognized for the appropriation and transmission—simultaneously—of another's words . . . 'reciting by heart' and 'retelling in one's own words'" (341). These basic modes became the primary stylistic means by which the observer was able to tell her own story while, ostensibly, adhering to and complying with her superiors' directives. By combining these two modes or by alternating between them, the observer was able to fulfill her duties as observer without compromising her own opinions and beliefs. In the transcripts, when she is "reciting by heart," she is preserving intact authoritative discourse; she is unable or unwilling to transform it in any way. When she is "retelling in her own words," she is involved in an expressive endeavor that goes beyond transmission and finds itself in the realm of representation.

In studying the transcripts of our taped interviews, it becomes clear that the observer is trying to accommodate the opposing voices of authoritative discourse which call for observations to be both collaborative and evaluative. Among the many and conflicting instructions for observations given by the observer's supervisor are the following: (1) she is to "help the instructor in classroom problem solving"; (2) she is to talk to the instructor "about your observations"; (3) she is not to form or make "conclusions or evaluations." At the same time, however, it is important to remember that the observers were working under guidelines that implicitly called for evaluation. If an observer is trained to focus on student and teacher interaction or questioning strategies, for example, it seems unlikely that these practices would not be measured or gauged in some way and that an observer would not speak of questioning strategies as effective or ineffective, or interesting or dull. Thus, an evaluation would be made whether an observer or supervisor wished to or not.

In the following example, the observer tries valiantly to follow the spirit of collaboration and to prove that complete collaboration has taken place between herself and the teacher. It is important to note a significant stylistic point of interest in the observer's narrative. There is a subtle shifting between the "I" and "she" of the story. When this shift occurs, the proximity of the observer to the instructor reveals the observer's attempt to reconcile the language of evaluation with the language of collaborative neutrality, which expressly forbids evaluation. In a kind of summary statement about a particular observation, the observer says:

> She [the teacher] picked out the weaknesses that I was going to point out. She knew that her discussion of literary devices would have been more effective if she had brought in specific examples. She did that in her second class, and it was much higher; she had much better success.

It is interesting to note that this passage is in a hypothetical mode. It seems that the observer never actually pointed out the weakness but that the teacher anticipated her thoughts, and in a kind of perfect mental communion, read her mind and knew what she would say, had she said it. Between these two speakers, internally persuasive discourse is being enacted, which Bakhtin describes as being "affirmed through assimilation, tightly interwoven with 'one's own word' . . . the internally persuasive word is half-ours and half-someone else's" (345).

This type of collaboration, once established, serves the observer well. She has not violated the spirit of the authoritative discourse: "To help the instructor in classroom problem solving." She has talked to the teacher as instructed, "about your observations." And she has not violated the injunction against "conclusions or evaluations," since she did not evaluate. The teacher simply said exactly what the observer would have said, had she spoken. The perfect melding of the author's and the teacher's words has taken place. Both observer and teacher are telling the same story.

In addition to complying with and promoting the idea of collaboration, the observer quickly finds that in her role of storyteller, she can begin to oppose the surrounding context of authoritative discourse. It is necessary that she do so because she is being asked to do something to which she is opposed. In the disadvantageous position of a teaching assistant, however, the ways in which she can oppose authoritative discourse are limited. She cannot approach her supervisor and tell her that she does not want to comply with a directive. Part of the observation rubric being followed during this time asked observers to do the following:

> Make a seating chart showing teacher and student activity . . . note gender as well as culture, race . . .

The observer responds to this directive and, at first, seems to comply. She mentions being struck by the fact that during group work, all the men seemed to sit together, and all the women seemed to sit together in a corner. She suggests to the teacher that she try shifting the students around to achieve a greater mix of gender and race. The teacher resists, saying that this would seem unnatural at this point in the semester. The word "unnatural," first uttered by the teacher, is given expression through the observer's speech:

> And she, she, you know, I, I don't know. I'm still very divided on that issue myself—to make sure that you don't have groups that are all men or all women, if it's important to divide them up somehow, to have a better mixture. I don't know if it's that important. I don't know how effective that would be.

Immediately after the word "unnatural" is uttered, it triggers a reaction in the observer. Her discourse is shaped in such a way as to argue internally against the intervention (suggesting a realignment of groups to the teacher), which the noting of gender, culture, and race seems to imply. She does not say that she doubts the effectiveness of having mixed groups; rather, she says that she doubts whether it is important "that you don't have groups that are all men or all women." It seems, since she chooses to question whether the negation or elimination of these groups would be effective, that she may, in fact, see this configuration as the norm, the "natural" way people may choose to group themselves, were it not for questionable intervention practices mandated by her supervisor.

This explains what may be termed the ideological conflict between authoritative discourse and the observer's discourse. But as with the first example, there is another dimension to be explored: How this ideological conflict is represented is of equal importance. Bakhtin speaks of hybridization, "the mixing of accents and erasing of boundaries between authorial speech and the speech of others." He says that the speech of characters may "overlap and infect each other" (320). Usually, Bakhtin is describing boundaries that lack syntactical divisions, and usually mixing of speeches is accomplished on a much more subtle level than the example given above. Yet, I think Bakhtin's definition of hybrid constructions is a useful one and one which can be applied here. There is an extraordinary degree of identification between observer and teacher in this excerpt. We have seen how the idea of "unnaturalness" has been appropriated by the observer, and it is reasonable to assume that had the teacher been given a voice beyond the word "unnatural," she, too, might have expressed the same opinion regarding seating arrangements. The observer's statement and the teacher's seem to have infected each other. But this example, unlike Bakhtin's, has syntactical markers. The observer says, "And she, she, you know, I, I" in a gesture to differentiate speakers, but the attempt is not entirely successful. The repetition of "she" and "I" indicates the difficulty experienced by the observer in effecting separation. However, if her intention is to gain an ally in opposition to authoritative discourse, separation would not be desirable. Perhaps she intends to have two speakers united in one discourse. If the observer and the teacher are telling the same story, if the "she" and "I" of the story have become one, perhaps their voices can be merged in opposition to the surrounding context of authoritative discourse, insisting as it does that they do something to which they are both opposed. Observers were told to record certain physical details of the classroom, and while these details are supposed to be simply objectively recorded, it seems that something in the directive, perhaps the "hidden" agenda or hint that this observation might yield documentation of some sociological import, unsettles both the teacher and the observer.

I do not mean to imply that the observer was working in a dictatorship where discussion and debate were forbidden and where dissension was not tolerated. This was not the case at all. Discussion about observation methods was encouraged, and suggestions for change were always taken into consideration. But what is important is that the teaching assistant observer did not feel that she could voice any opposition. Because of her inferior position, she was simply unable to express her opinions openly. Instead, she chose to ally herself with another teaching assistant, the observed, and to express her opposition in an oblique way through her narrative of the observation. Of course, it is impossible to know what the teacher said to the observer, and it is true that what we know about the observer's experience is a representation of the observation, one version of what took place. What this example reveals, more than any presumption that "truth" is being uncovered, is the degree to which the teaching assistant feels powerless. It is likely that the teaching assistant's supervisor never perceived this feeling of powerlessness and that she acted in good faith while overseeing observers. Without an act of reflexivity, such as the meta-ethnography about which I report, asymmetries of power, albeit unintentional, would continue to exist. To prove that the supervisor was not interested in perpetuating these asymmetrical power relations, and in fairness to her, I must point out that it was she who suggested the meta-ethnography of the basic writing program's observation mechanism. What was revealed was that teaching assistants find their hands tied on several accounts.

In many cases, teaching assistants have to pay allegiance to many masters. They must perform outstandingly as students and scholars to maintain their positions as teaching assistants. They must do what they are told to do in the classroom while teaching, at the same time exhibiting a superior level of competency or a spark of individuality or creativity that sets them apart from their fellow teaching assistants. Juggling these various tasks enables them to move into more desirable teaching assignments and situations.

Another complicating factor, perhaps one of the most crucial, must be acknowledged. The observer whom I studied served as both mentor and formal observer. The lines of authority between her and her charge became easily blurred. She was called upon to act as mentor, to develop a fruitful, trusting relationship with her junior teaching assistant, but she was also told to act as a formal observer and to report to, or to put it more neutrally, confer with, the person who supervises teaching assistants. It seems to me that everyone's position is put in jeopardy in a situation such as this. Even when something is said off the record, or in the spirit of constructive criticism, with the best of intentions, that statement makes an indelible impression on the ear and mind of the supervisor. This impression may not find itself in the teaching assistant's file, transformed into an official evaluation, but the impression has been made, and its impact should not be underestimated or diminished. Sometime in the future, when choice teaching assignments are being made or when names are being tossed about to fill a job opening, this impression may be given voice and may find a listener. Clearly, much can ride on an unofficial comment. Imagine, then, the weight of an official evaluative report and the impulse by some to avoid evaluation or to pretend that it is not a part of the classroom observation.

Without constant self-examination and without the kind of self-reflexive strategies described by Gary L. Anderson (1989) and others, it is impossible to ascertain how well any enterprise is functioning. In the case of classroom observations, with their high stakes and with their implications for both teachers and students, it is of the utmost importance that methods for self-evaluation be developed and practiced. A meta-ethnography containing several levels of observation, combined with various media of observation, ranging from field notes to taped interviews, to transcripts and narratives about observations, yields interesting and comprehensive data.

I would like to dip once more into the record to illustrate what I believe to be the observer's most sophisticated attempt to reconcile the conflict between collaboration and evaluation. In this example it is also clear that the lines between objectivity and subjectivity are becoming blurred in this confused observation context. The observer encounters a situation that absolutely begs for correction, but she is caught between authoritative discourse, which instructs the observer to simply record and remain objective, and her own subjective interpretation of these details. Instructions to the observer read as follows:

> In the field notes record that is on the board, describe the classroom artifacts, and note what happens as the instructor and students enter the room. An objective collection of data at this point is what you are interested in.

In the observation that is the focus of my interest, I found that the observer was concerned not so much by the entrance of students, but rather, by the exits; to be more precise, it was the coming and going of the students, a topic that dominated much of the postobservation interview. Here, the observer refers to one particular student who came in five minutes after roll was taken, immediately asked to leave to get his paper from his car, and returned to class ten minutes later:

> So I didn't know what, you know. That was just something I pointed out. I pointed this out to her [the teacher]. I don't know if I would have let him leave, but this is not my class. So I thought it was important to show her that this was disruptive. I mean, I was distracted. It was hard for me to pay attention for . . . right after he left, I was like, "Where is he going, what is he doing, why does he get to leave?"

It is clear that the observer is still trying to negotiate between the objective record of the class that merely documents the fact that students (this was not the only one) were coming and going during class, and her subjective reaction to these incidents. The observer is grappling with the problem of telling the teacher that this is unacceptable without using evaluative terms. She makes the disclaimer that this is not her class, but it is impossible for her to distance herself from this incident; she is in extremely close proximity to the teacher, so close, in fact, that her almost complete identification with the teacher is taking place.

Bakhtin claims that there is an "arena for the encounter" between the speaker and the "subjective belief system of the listener" (282). Here, I think, the arena of encounter is between the observer and the teacher and between the charge to be objective, spoken in the authoritative discourse, and the difficulty of doing so when an event collides with one's subjective belief system. The encounter takes place and is over-shadowed by the observer's transmission of authoritative discourse—"this is not my class"—but the observer attempts to move beyond transmission to representation. Even though the quotation is syntacti-cally marked—"I was like" introduces it as the author's words—there is a particular presentness to it. Whose words appear at the end of the passage? A voice says, "Where is he going, what is he doing, why does he get to leave?" It is as though the observer is suddenly back in the classroom, speaking in the present tense, acting as teacher and asking the questions she would have asked had she been in front of the classroom with the authority to ask those questions. Or these could be the questions that the author of a novel would have a character speak, since she could populate the character's speech with her own inten-tions. The words of the observer and the teacher could be uttered in the same space. The antagonistic relationship between objectivity and subjectivity is thus temporarily dissolved. If the observer can speak in the teacher's place, she is speaking as the teacher would speak. She now has permission to be subjective, since she and the teacher share one subjectivity.

These examples represent just some of the observer's attempts to negotiate her way between two contradictory discourses. On another level, they also represent her attempts to both appropriate and transmit the teacher's words, to recall the story by heart and to tell the story in her own words. On yet another level, if we claim that the observer's retelling is a fictional, novel-like construction, we may say that conscious hybridization between author (observer) and character (teacher) has taken place. The observer is involved in an expressive endeavor that goes beyond transmission and finds itself in the realm of representation, replete with characters who may either express her views or who may, at her behest, find voices that are capable of expressing their own intentions and ideologies. The language of the observation is not a unitary language, with transparent authorial intentions, nor is it independent of other languages; instead, it is one of many languages, arrested for a time within a particular context. It is striving to do work, to say something; it is willing to accommodate other voices, but unwilling to silence itself.

When the observer witnessed unauthorized movement in and out of the class, she was compelled to stop being objective and to tell the teacher that this movement was "disruptive." This is a pejorative term, and it certainly involves evaluation. Although I believe that what the observer had to say was certainly within the bounds of collaboration, she felt that she had violated the spirit of collaboration, hence the need to identify so strongly with the teacher. At first, she engages in an elaborate attempt to separate herself from the teacher—"This is not my class"—but the effort collapses into the almost complete appropriation of the teacher's role. The observer speaks in place of the teacher—"Where is he going, what is he doing, why does he get to leave?" This incident raises important questions about collaboration and evaluation. All observers face this dilemma, whether observers are teaching assistants or senior faculty. On the one hand, an observer has to allay the fears of a teacher and put her at ease in order for a teacher to be able to at least approximate what happens on an ordinary day in her classroom. If an observer is also a mentor, she must give honest criticism and support to a teacher and also build a relationship based on trust and respect. But if an observer and mentor is also called upon to evaluate, the relationship becomes too complicated to handle.

One way to simplify the observation and to eliminate confusion about the purpose of observations is to create a two-tiered or a multitiered observation system. In order to foster true collaboration, a system has to be created whereby teachers of equal rank visit each other. These visits are in no way supervisory and no written record of the visits is ever produced. Teaching assistants, for example, visit each other offering impressions and suggestions while learning much about their own teaching through the transaction. Anyone who has observed knows that one of the positive by-products of observing is that the observer herself can become a better teacher. Observers are exposed to a wealth of new ideas, methods, and strategies for teaching, and they often get to see the shape of courses or the way in which a teacher conceptualizes the aims of a course and the way in which she paces the development of a course.

Observers' impressions and judgments, even about equals, cannot be eliminated, nor should they be. A discerning human always sorts, categorizes, and ranks experience. Conclusions will be drawn about what has been seen and heard, but peer observation does not enter the official written record. Unofficial evaluation will take place, but since everyone acts as both observer and observed, decorous habits of observation develop. In other words, everyone gets his or her turn, so it pays to be encouraging, helpful, and polite.

Another method of equalizing observations is to engage in self-observation through videotaping. By videotaping I do not mean the static, staged, scripted training films to which we have all been subjected. Instead, I mean live classroom performances, recorded with a moving camera that catches interaction between teacher and students and among students by means of closeups, zooms, and so on and by a camera that covers the entire classroom, not just a medium shot of a teacher standing behind a desk talking to disembodied student voices. Teachers have the opportunity to view their performances in private and make necessary adjustments. Videotapes can be viewed over and over, and an observer can read a videotape in much the same way that any text is read, that is, for different levels of meaning. She can discover the verbal and nonverbal patterns that emerge and also the various languages or discourses that exist within the classroom. The methods that I have employed in analyzing an observer's reaction to an observation can be used by a teacher when she reviews the videotaped record of her performance. Teachers need to be trained to read the videotape in depth, but this can be accomplished fairly easily by reviewing and discussing tapes in a teaching practicum or in a workshop.

When teachers visit and are visited by their peers, collaboration does ensue. In addition, anxiety about having a stranger in the classroom is reduced, thus preparing the way for a smoother evaluative observation. It would be foolish of me to pretend that being observed by a peer and being observed by an evaluator for purposes of financial aid, fellowships, promotion and tenure is the same thing. It is not, and one should not be lulled into thinking that it is. The stakes are higher and the dangers are greater when one is being evaluated, but a teacher's chances of being comfortable with someone else in the classroom are greatly increased through peer observation, and the invaluable feedback from peers prior to an evaluative observation surely produces better classroom performances.

I began with a call to look at observations critically and to explore the ways in which the critical viewer herself is implicated in and contributes to the complex process of observing and evaluating another's performance. I am aware that as an interviewer of an observer, I added yet another dimension to a multivocal context.* I became another speaker, another listener, and another author. Undoubtedly, my single presence performed many functions. I was construed as an authority figure, yet I became a co-conspirator with the observer. Just as she allied herself with the teacher against authoritative discourse, she allied herself with me and I with her. I became the vehicle for her story and the voice which told what had to be told. I am not quite sure how this transference of power was accomplished, but at some point, I arranged a coup of my own. I appropriated her voice; I presumed to speak for her. I fell prey to the same temptation to transform another's story into my own story, using it for my own purposes. But the stories told are real—real representations of reality—and what they reveal needs to be told.

The confusion surrounding the purpose of the observation has to be eliminated. Those in charge of supervising observations must decide whether they wish to collaborate or evaluate or both. As I have illustrated, if one person is charged with both collaboration and evaluation, neither component of the observation can be executed effectively, and neither can be carried out openly or completely. Supervisors must acknowledge the forces operating within the observation context and address questions of race, class, gender, and power relations. Only by establishing clear objectives for observations and by demystifying the observation process through training teachers to be observers of themselves—looking for the same things that we trained observers look for—can we hope to make observations the fair and useful tools for improving teaching that we wish them to be and that they are, indeed, supposed to be.

Works Cited

Anderson, Gary L. 1989. "Critical Ethnography in Education: Origins, Current Status, and New Directions." *Review of Educational Research* 59: 249–70.

---

* I thank Frank Sullivan for suggesting that I observe myself, as well.

Bakhtin, M. M. 1981. *The Dialogic Imagination: Four Essays.* Edited by Michael Holquist. Translated by Caryl Emerson and Michael Holquist. Austin: University of Texas Press.

Brodkey, Linda. 1987. "Writing Ethnographic Narratives." *Written Communication* 4: 25–50.

7 (E)VALUE(D): When Writing Teachers Teach Literature

Michael J. Vivion
University of Missouri at Kansas City

Until recently, I had accepted peer evaluation as an inevitable academic ritual, something that was, is, and always will be. I regularly endured it and its accompanying anxiety, hoping that those who visited my classes would like what they saw.

I was the director of composition for my first nine years at the University of Missouri at Kansas City, and during those nine years, my peers evaluated my performance as a teacher of literature only once. Each subsequent evaluation focused on my teaching of writing. The peers who evaluated me were tenured members of the literature faculty; not one taught composition. Consequently, the hierarchic nature of the evaluation had been inverted. I was the *peer* among peers, the *director* who could do no wrong, because the evaluators had little notion of what I was doing and even less of how well I was doing it.

I was also a director of composition who had come into the field the "old" way, with a Ph.D. in literature and with many years of experience teaching composition as a high school teacher and as a teaching assistant. I have been told that I got the position directing composition at UMKC because of the combination of my literature background and composition interest. As the story goes, the composition staff, at that time all part-time lecturers, voted against hiring me; they perceived me as the literature candidate who would even do composition if it meant getting a job. On the other hand, the "regular" faculty appreciated my potential, seeing me as a fellow colleague in literature with a slight eccentricity manifested by an interest in composition. The department and I have survived this tension quite well and with great mutual tolerance over the last nine years. Recently, however, two separate incidents helped me rediscover the fragility of the institutional balance between composition and literature and brought my feelings about peer evaluation into a sharper, more critical focus. They also renewed my memory of a third incident, one which had led me to the composition program at UMKC in the first place.

In this chapter, I plan to use these three incidents to introduce a discussion of the issue of peer evaluation in a field struggling with conflicting values, in particular between those of an established literature faculty and those of an emerging composition faculty. The incidents themselves are presented neither as archetypal nor as definitive, but rather as examples of what can happen when oranges evaluate tangerines for structure and content in order to establish the worth of the individual tangerine.

The issue of evaluation demands our attention because the current structure of many, if not most, of our English departments privileges literature both in the number of regular faculty and in their respective levels of prestige. In some English departments, faculty designated as writing teachers are also assigned to teach in other areas, usually literature. In other cases, recent literature Ph.D.s are hired to teach literature but to bring with them the teaching philosophies and practices they developed as teaching assistants within composition programs. In both of these situations, teaching evaluations are mostly performed by senior literature faculty. Furthermore, tenure-track composition professors are frequently evaluated by these same senior literature faculty. In all three scenarios, those who are less likely to be familiar with the current reading/writing pedagogy being developed within the field of composition are entrusted with the evaluative power.

Many of our professional discussions about the power structure of English departments focus on the split between composition and literature. In these discussions, as in Bullock and Trimbur's *The Politics of Writing Instruction: Postsecondary* (1991), the disparities which receive the most attention are salary, status, publication, gender, teaching load, teaching assistants, and other issues related to university and departmental politics. Even when the discussion turns to the difficulties composition teachers face in the tenure and promotion process, however, as it does in Charles Schuster's essay "The Politics of Promotion," in the same volume, the issue of the evaluation process is conspicuously absent. We need to explore how the split between composition and literature can affect evaluation so that we can develop a process which allows for differences and which encourages faculty to improve teaching.

In the best of situations, the concept of "peer evaluation" is oxymoronic. The term *peer* suggests a certain equality; the term *evaluation* reveals a functioning hierarchy. The contradiction is especially noteworthy when the "peer evaluation" occurs within the contexts of tenure, promotion, and merit raises. In these contexts, nontenured faculty are much more threatened by this system than senior faculty—although when raises and promotions include peer evaluations and when these evaluating peers serve on the promotion and salary committees, the pressure can be increased on senior faculty as well. Nontenured faculty, however, can feel real pressure to change the ways they teach in order to meet the expectations of their evaluating peers.

In the situations I have described, there is a dual hierarchy at work. We see the hierarchy of evaluator/evaluated, but we should also recognize the hierarchy of discipline: literary/nonliterary, privileged/marginalized. The dynamics of the second hierarchy are marked by potential conflicts between the current-traditional values sometimes held by senior literature faculty and the less traditional values held by those educated in contemporary composition pedagogy, thus creating a situation in which those who are being evaluated can become disempowered as decision-making professionals. Seen in this context, the issue of evaluation is clearly one of values and leads to an important question: What values are embedded within evaluation?

The memory prompted by the two recent incidents is of a moment earlier in my career, at another university. I was a tenure-track, new Ph.D. teaching the undergraduate English methods course for future secondary teachers. During the second year of my appointment, one of the senior literature faculty requested of the chair the opportunity to teach the graduate-level methods course. His reason: "To counter some of the soft-headed theories which were being peddled" in the undergraduate course. The soft-headed theories he had in mind were the writing process and reader-response criticism. He believed writing to be a series of rules skillfully applied and literature, a set of texts and historical facts to be learned. The fact that this senior professor played an important role in the evaluation process for tenure and promotion led me to an early career decision: to look for a department more hospitable to my own values. At that time, I considered this conflict in values to be a personal one. In fact, I basically wrote off his response as one generated by an isolated curmudgeon. I failed then to recognize the importance of our conflict to the entire profession and to the processes of evaluation.

The first of the two recent incidents was the peer evaluation of one of my friends, a new Ph.D. hired to teach literature at a state university.* While working on her Ph.D., she participated in a graduate assistant educational program that emphasized active learning and introduced ideas common to both contemporary composition theory and liberatory pedagogy. Out of this experience she had developed a technique for using the student reading journal in her literature courses. She would open the approach to a work with a read-around during which the

---

* Some of the details have been changed to protect the privacy of both my colleague and the university involved.

students would read and respond to each other's journals, ideally with little teacher interference. The goals motivating this approach are that the students will engage with the text, that they will make connections be- tween the text and their lives, that they will engage with each other about the disparities among their responses, and that they will become empowered as readers—and writers—without the primary, direct intervention of the teacher.

The peer evaluator who visited her class and saw this approach in action came away with several strong reservations. He was concerned that the instructor had not "corrected" some of the "off-the-wall" statements that the students made. He was concerned that the literary text had not received more direct attention. He was concerned that the instructor had not "controlled" the class. In the follow-up conversation, the evaluator made it clear that the cause for these "mistakes" was probably the instructor's lack of experience.

The instructor, on the other hand, felt that the class session had been one of the most successful of the year. The students had argued about the text's meaning. They had argued the correctness of the text's assertions. They had contested each other's interpretations. They had used their own experiences to support their opinions and their readings.

When the evaluator returned for a second visit, he came away pleased. This time the instructor had controlled the class, taking the students through the text more closely, directing their reading and their comprehension. This class, she felt—but did not tell her evaluator—was less successful than the earlier class. The difference between the two class sessions, she told me, was due partially to her desire to show her evaluator what he wanted. She had, however, another reason for the change in her approach: the surface features of the second text were more difficult than those of the first, warranting a different approach. The nature of the text had caused her to change her approach.

The second incident sharpening my criticism of peer review was my own. Peer evaluation is part of the promotion process. When I was reviewed for promotion from assistant to associate professor, memory tells me that the process was smooth. My classes, both composition and literature, had been observed early in my employment. The literature faculty had judged that I could teach literature and trusted that I could teach composition. The composition program was thriving and developing, and so was I; somewhere along the way, like many of us in composition, I had undergone major changes in my view of our profession and how we teach.

As it turned out, neither of the groups involved in my hiring was correct. I have learned to consider myself a professor of English studies interested in the production and reception of texts, and as such, during any given class period, whether in a composition course or a literature course, it is difficult to tell if I'm teaching production or reception, writing or reading, composition or literature.

Now I am being considered for promotion to full professor. Now evaluation is a problem; not because the department isn't going to put me forward, because it is, even with enthusiasm, I think. The problem is that this time one of my literature courses was chosen for evaluation, and along with the recommendation for promotion will go the letters my colleagues wrote about my teaching, at least one of which brings up one of the questions which motivates this chapter: How will literature faculty evaluate the next generation of scholars rising out of teaching assistant programs that emphasize reading/writing connections and that teach techniques and approaches which blur disciplinary lines?

The class being evaluated was a junior-level survey of American literature from the Civil War to World War II; we were working on a group of Robert Frost's poems. There were two student reports, one on Midwestern attitudes toward nature and one on Frost's personal and problematic experiences in nature. Excerpts from the evaluation written by my peer, a member of the literature faculty, follow:

> The hour began . . . with a student report on the image of the Middle West in the late 19th century. The report went on long past its allotted five minutes and never did make clear its connection with Frost, a New Englander, but Vivion, I suppose on principle, made no effort to interrupt. [*Moving now to comments on the two foci of the "teaching" of the poems: persona and the nature of nature:*] As the students identified characteristics of the persona or poems that illustrated them, Vivion listed them on the blackboard. At times it seemed difficult for the students to consider the assignment as a whole (the page-turning was sometimes deafening) but the main ideas eventually emerged. The second theme [*the nature of nature*] presented a different difficulty because Vivion, in trying to relate Frost's view of nature to Emerson's or Thoreau's, discovered that almost none of the students knew anything at all about them. A good deal of time seemed to be spent on discovering this, and he ended up telling them anyway. In any case, very little of the hour was devoted to close reading of individual passages, a serious handicap, I believe, in the teaching of poetry. [*Some final comments:*] . . . (He later told me that students in groups do research and they argue for the right to add their writer to the syllabus.) . . . Although I would do almost everything differently, I suspect that the students learn a great deal in Vivion's classes and probably enjoy the experience.

The three incidents I have isolated illustrate some of the perils inherent in peer evaluation. Instruction is epistemology. Teachers make decisions, either implicitly or explicitly, about the nature of knowledge and the nature of knowing—about what is worth knowing and the ways of knowing. Other important decisions are based on ideology. When evaluations do not acknowledge the epistemological nature of teaching, a strong possibility exists for dissonance, for misevaluating, for not seeing what is actually happening in the classroom, or for not seeing it for what it's supposed to be. In other words, there is a strong possibility that it is, indeed, not our teaching which is being evaluated, but rather, the belief and value systems which drive our teaching. And when the literature/composition dichotomy is invoked, the clash of values calls into question the validity of any conclusions drawn. I believe that the three incidents I have cited indicate clearly that conflicting values do influence the nature of evaluation. In the final section of this essay, I will return to the incidents and demonstrate what I perceive to be the conflicts.

Before I do this, I should offer two qualifications. First, I fully realize that the techniques, approaches, and epistemologies I present as representative of composition are not solely the result of work within composition. Many of them developed independently within the general area of liberatory pedagogy; others developed out of the intellectual fervor associated with contemporary forms of literary criticism. In other words, it is quite possible that English professors teaching within a nontraditional framework would also experience difficulties when they are evaluated by current-traditional literature faculty.

Nevertheless, I would assert that the writing process movement served as a catalyst for experimentation within English studies, experimentation which led to the acceptance of a widely divergent range of approaches within composition. I would also assert that composition's marginalization within English studies creates an atmosphere in which professors associated with composition and its approaches to teaching are more suspect than even the most radical literature professors. Further intensifying this suspicion is the willingness, even eagerness, of those associated with composition to talk and to write about teaching. In my experience of teaching at four universities, only the composition faculty were willing to devote systematic time to and preparation for discussion of pedagogy.

The second qualification has to do with the nature of values within composition itself. It is quite likely that those compositionists who accept the values underlying the current-traditional model of composition would find themselves more comfortable with the values which both Schuster and I assign to the senior literature faculty. Rather than invalidating my position, however, this recognition of conflicting values within the composition field itself illustrates how problematic the whole issue of peer evaluation really is.

In most of my courses, both composition and literature, I give some direct attention to oral language. In my literature courses, I create activities which require students to organize their thoughts orally. For example, I frequently provide students with the opportunity to talk through their essays before they begin to write, calling on the talk/write approach to prewriting. Students participate in a variety of group discussions, using techniques I learned in my composition courses. They then summarize the contents and processes of their deliberations. They give formal reports on historical, cultural, and ideological topics, reports whose purpose is to add a level of funding to their classmates' reading of literature or to show how their research affected the way they read a particular piece. I ask for reading journals or freewriting to be read aloud. I structure classroom discussion so that every student participates.

I also use techniques I have developed out of my research into the reading/writing connection. I accept and explore the idea that there are reading processes that can be taught. For example, I ask students to keep reading journals which I sometimes use to begin classes. The journals receive random comments related to content but no marks on mechanics, grammar, or usage. Sometimes I ask students to freewrite in class if I think they are having trouble with a piece or if they need to refocus. I ask students to predict the content and direction of fiction at various stages in their reading. I ask them to identify with characters. I ask them to write new endings for fiction. I ask them to imitate poetic patterns, experiment with points of view, create tropes. Occasionally I accept their own literary efforts in lieu of essays.

I also use groups in a variety of ways. As mentioned earlier, groups meet to collaborate during various stages of their writing processes. They also meet to collaborate on interpretation. Sometimes all the groups work on the same piece and bring the results of their collaboration back to the large group for collective discussion. Sometimes, however, the group is responsible for the entire presentation of a piece to the entire class. Most idiosyncratic to my literature colleagues, however, is when groups meet to decide issues related to the content of the syllabus. Whereas my composition classes decide which issues to discuss and then bring articles to class, my literature classes regularly decide which pieces we will cover. For example, this past semester each group presented a poem to the entire class with the task of convincing them that its poem should be studied in depth. From the six poems presented, the class chose one.

Few composition teachers would find what I have described as being unique to my teaching or even unusual. Schuster (1991) provides an insightful assessment of why literature faculty might evaluate these classes with some dismay:

> Whereas many literature faculty define the classroom as an authoritarian field of inquiry in which professors maintain a privileged speaking role while students learn primarily through listening and imitating, composition faculty create collaborative classrooms and writing workshops, thereby undercutting the traditional professorial power structure. As a result of these differences, English department literary faculty often look upon their compositional brothers and sisters an incompetent, idiosyncratic, confused, valueless, untenurable. (85–86)

The evaluations explicit in Schuster's words—"incompetent, idiosyncratic, confused, valueless, untenurable"—are remarkably similar to the attitudes expressed in the three incidents I have cited: "soft-headed," "inexperienced," "would do almost everything differently."

The primary epistemological conflict I see in the three examples is related to the process/product dichotomy. The literature professors assert the New Critical view that knowledge exists; and in the literature course, the locus of the knowledge is within the text. Students attain this knowledge through a strong engagement with the surface features of a text, thereby leading to an interpretation. Ideologically, these professors believe that the authority for the interpretation resides in the text and that their role is either to provide the knowledge, an accepted interpretation, or to correct any imperfect interpretation which might result from a faulty engagement with the text. They also tend to believe that a superior form of knowledge exists, thereby positing a well-defined canon. This description of current-traditional literary practices is not new; however, when it is applied to classroom activities it reveals the potential for a low tolerance of teaching that moves the text from the center of study, that diminishes the authority of the professor, and that takes time away from a thorough coverage of the canon—all of which are likely to be exhibited by a colleague applying contemporary composition theory and practice.

This colleague is likely to be operating within a different structure of beliefs and values. In contemporary composition, knowledge is problematic, an interactive construct. Compositionists tend to pay attention to the reasons students construct and receive texts the way they do. They explore the relationships between competence and performance, realizing that reading and writing are not fixed skills which can be applied consistently in every communication task. They explore rhetorical contexts, cultural causation, cognitive development. They value experience as a proof, a form of evidence. They believe that this dynamic knowledge is best taught interactively; they do not believe in teaching by exhortation. They believe that students, in order to learn, must have ownership of their texts—including interpretation. They believe that authority is earned, demonstrated, and shared. They believe that time spent learning processes, rather than a canon, is not time wasted. This view of the differences between instruction in literature and in composition is depressingly polarized. On the other hand, we do have the precedent within our profession of accepting difference. With a few notable exceptions, the status of the journal article as part of the evaluation process provides us, at least in the departments I've been in, with a place to meet. If it is publishable in a refereed journal, then an article must have some worth—even if we might privately consider it "idiosyncratic" or even "confused." We can generally agree on this evaluation even though we know that when we submit professional essays to journals, we choose a journal on the basis of its potential receptivity to our topic and, often, to our ideas. We may, at times, submit an essay which challenges the journal's epistemological and ideological assumptions, but we nevertheless assume that the journal's editor will understand the reasons for our assertions. The dissenting essay is published to encourage dialogue. This same principle should hold true for the evaluation processes. Just as there are a variety of journals in our field of English studies, there are, in teaching, a variety of beliefs, values, and approaches. We can learn to accept divergence if we change the way we think about evaluating teaching.

There is no doubt that we will continue to evaluate teaching. If we want teaching ever to be awarded the status which research and publication receive, we must evaluate it with the same rigor. (How well we truly evaluate research and publication is a question for another essay.) To do this, we must create a process which foregrounds epistemology and ideology. In such a department, the teachers' beliefs about the nature and processes of knowing would be a common topic for formal and informal discussion. Discussions about the values underlying the curriculum would be common. Epistemological and ideological differences would be recognized and celebrated in colloquia and in the department's various course offerings as part of the hermeneutic function of an English department.

Our department tries to send peer evaluators into classes which they themselves teach or have taught. In addition, we are encouraged to solicit syllabi and a general description of the topic for the day. We do not, however, either formally or informally, discuss what it is that we want our students to know or how we think that they can come to this knowledge. As a result, when we do a class evaluation, we can only use as a standard our own epistemology. In a reformed evaluation system, no visitation would occur without a preliminary discussion which would begin with a series of questions focusing on beliefs, values, and implementation: *What do you want your students to learn? Why is it important for them to learn this thing (fact) (process) (value) (concept)? What do you plan to do to facilitate that learning?* Similarly, the discussions after classroom visitations would end with a series of questions: *What do you think your students learned? How will you know? What will you do differently next time?* We should also, lest we be accused of Orwellian doublespeak, change the name of this process from peer evaluation to something like departmental evaluation.

If we also want this process we heretofore have been calling evaluation to become a means through which we can improve teaching, then we need to create a process which complements departmental evaluation. In our new enlightened department, evaluation would be reformulated as peer consultation or as peer collaboration, and it should be part of the discursive practices mentioned in the previous paragraph. In both evaluation and collaboration, we should recognize differences in pedagogy as intellectual dialectic rather than as questions of competence. This reformed department would reflect the intellectual fervor that Gerald Graff describes in *Professing Literature* (1987) but would engage both composition and literature professors in the dialectic as suggested by Christy Friend (1992) in her recent essay on Graff's book.

In *What Is English?* Peter Elbow (1990) defines the limits of evaluation: "even though nothing can remove the deep epistemological fragility that surrounds any interpretation or claim to knowledge, nevertheless we can have an evaluation that, though not sure, is at least something that we need not be ashamed of" (246). I believe that we can have greater expectations, higher goals than avoiding shame. We can develop processes of evaluation which allow us to establish nonhierarchical collegiality, and we can institute a collaboration which leads us toward more effective teaching.

Works Cited

Bullock, Richard H., and John Trimbur, eds. 1991. *The Politics of Writing Instruction: Postsecondary.* Portsmouth, NH: Boynton/Cook.

Elbow, Peter. 1990. *What Is English?* New York: Modern Language Association of America; Urbana: National Council of Teachers of English.

Friend, Christy. 1992. "The Excluded Conflict: The Marginalization of Composition and Rhetoric Studies in Graff's *Professing Literature.*" *College English* 54: 276–86.

Graff, Gerald. 1987. *Professing Literature: An Institutional History.* Chicago: University of Chicago Press.

Schuster, Charles I. 1991. "The Politics of Promotion." In Bullock and Trimbur, 85–95.

8 Making Better Use of Student Evaluations of Teachers

Peter Elbow
University of Massachusetts at Amherst

I hear widespread skepticism about students as evaluators of teachers:

> Students are immature and not yet educated and don't know about teaching and learning as we do.

> Students just go on feelings, what they like, what's fun or entertaining; they can be seduced by a good show and easy grades.

> Student estimations of teachers vary wildly all over the map; their evaluations obviously have no reliability.

What shall we conclude from these charges? What I conclude is this: we feel the problems of evaluation more keenly when we are on the receiving end than when we are on the giving end. That is, the charges I've just summarized simply throw more light on the problems in *all* evaluation, particularly conventional faculty grading of students. Let me set the problems of student evaluations into a larger context by looking briefly at evaluation in general.

Trustworthy, fair evaluation means giving God's verdict—finding the single verdict that all right-minded good readers would agree on. The problem is that God isn't telling her verdict, and we cannot get readers to agree—not even *good* readers. It may sound extreme to invoke God here, but we can't be cavalier about evaluation in education. A single student's evaluation of a teacher doesn't carry much weight, but a single teacher's grade for a student often carries a lot, e.g., for a scholarship or a job or professional school. We can't just give grades and take a fashionably theoretical view: "Oh well, of course my grades are 'situated' and 'interested'—so what else is new?" Because grades carry heavy consequences, we cannot take anything less than genuine fairness as our goal—God's view, correctness—yet we know that trustworthy, fair evaluation is not possible.

Reprinted by permission of the Modern Language Association of America from *ADE Bulletin* 101 (Spring 1992): 2–8. The present version is the author's revision of that piece.

I'm not saying anything new. We have long seen this on many fronts. Research in evaluation has repeatedly shown that if we give a paper to a set of readers, those readers tend to give it the full range of grades. (For a classic exploration, see Diederich 1974; for an indication of how long people have noticed this problem, see Starch and Elliott 1913; Kirschenbaum, Napier, and Simon 1971, 258–59.)

We know the same thing from literary criticism and theory. The best critics disagree about the quality of texts—even about what texts mean—and nothing in literary or philosophical theory gives us any agreed-upon rules for settling such disputes. Barbara Herrnstein Smith (1988) may not be too cynical in concluding that whenever we have interreader reliability, we have something fishy. And students know the same thing from their own controlled experiments of handing in the same paper to different teachers and getting different grades. (Perhaps this explains why we tend to hate it when students ask their favorite question, "What do you want for an A?": it rubs our noses in the unreliability of our grades.)

Champions of holistic scoring will reply that they *do* get readers to agree, but they get that agreement by "training" the readers before and during the scoring sessions, that is, getting them to stop using the conflicting criteria and standards they normally use outside the scoring session. Thus, the reliability in holistic scoring is not a measure of how texts are valued by actual readers in natural settings, but only of how they are valued in artificial settings with imposed agreements.

Despite these practical and theoretical problems, we can't scrap evaluation. Everyone seems to want teachers to evaluate students. And most people want students to evaluate teachers in some way. After all, colleges operate in a competitive marketplace where students are the consumers we need to survive. If we are selling a service, we can't say, "Who cares what consumers think?" We need students more than they need us; it's a buyer's market—they can always go elsewhere. Indeed, this asymmetry is also structural: students can learn without teachers, but teachers cannot teach without students.

So if fair, trustworthy evaluation is impossible but evaluation is necessary, what is the moral? I see only one answer: do it less; do it better.

Do It Less

Good evaluation is more work, but less evaluation would be a blessing. In particular, we can get along with much less high-stakes, institutional evaluation of teachers by students if we make more use of informal, unofficial feedback from them. I am thinking of the evaluation we get when we ask students to write letters or comments to us about what is helpful and not helpful in our teaching. This evaluation has much lower stakes because it is for our eyes alone. (We can also use comparable private, informal, low-stakes evaluation by a friendly colleague or by someone in a faculty development office.) We tend to learn and improve more on the basis of this kind of unofficial feedback because it is less threatening: we have more control over it and don't have to defend against it as much as we do against official institutional feedback. (I say this on the basis of having set up and been "visitor" in a faculty peer-feedback system; see Elbow 1986.)

When I ask students for this kind of informal evaluation, I like to do it at midsemester and make sure that they can feel this as a request from me as teacher, not from some larger impersonal institutional enterprise. Indeed, I often simply ask my students to write me a letter that answers questions like these: "What are the most important skills and contents you have learned? What skills or abilities do you see me most trying to teach? Which features of the course and my teaching have worked well and which ones not so well?" There are many benefits from this midsemester procedure: there is still time for improvement in that very semester. And the mere fact that I make the request improves my relationship with students: it encourages honesty and attention to teaching on their part and mine.

Even though this informal evaluation is private and noninstitutional, a department or chair or institution can, indeed should, make it happen—for example, by requiring faculty members to write periodic, reflective, self-evaluations of their teaching and asking that these documents discuss what they learned from the private evaluations from colleagues and students.

Someone might object that in a section entitled "Do It Less," I am calling for an awful lot of evaluation. True enough, but this informal evaluation is easy and nonbureaucratic, and it permits much less frequent institutional, high-stakes evaluation: perhaps only every two to three semesters for untenured faculty and every four to five semesters for tenured.

Do It Better

What would better evaluation look like? Above all, it would be more trustworthy and more informative. These two goals point straight at the main culprit in evaluation: fine-grained, holistic, numerical ranking along a single dimension. It is these alleged measurements of a complex performance—scorings from 1 to 5 or F to A—that are least trustworthy and informative. These laconic numbers are nothing but points along a yea/boo continuum—with no information about the criteria behind the yea's and boo's. They tell us with laughable precision how well or poorly evaluators think someone did, but nothing at all about what they meant by "well" or "poorly"—what they were looking at or looking for.

When we stop pretending to measure a complex performance along one numerical scale, we naturally bring in more useful evaluative information. That is, we are led to create student evaluations which focus on questions such as these: How well does this teacher conduct discussions, give lectures, help you understand the course concepts and information, devise assignments, comment on papers, help you learn to think for yourself, establish good relations with you, and so forth? Even if we are forced to ask for *numerical* answers to these questions because there are too many students to permit us to read written answers, we don't pretend we can add up these numbers and come up with a "score" for how good the teacher is. We realize that the results need interpretation.

What I am talking about here is the crucial distinction between *ranking* and *judging*. To rank is to give a single, holistic, numerical verdict along one dimension—even for a complex or multidimensional performance like teaching. To judge is to look carefully enough at the performance to distinguish among parts or features or dimensions and decide which parts of the teaching are more effective and which are less so. The process itself of judging, because it is discriminating or analytic, helps us acknowledge that different dimensions of the teaching will matter more to different students. For example, some students will see a good teacher as someone who gets the material across clearly and doesn't disturb their assumptions and routines. Other students will see a good teacher as someone who shakes things up and actually causes them to question their assumptions and routines.

So where ranking gives us nothing but a number, judging gives useful information about which features of the teaching worked better or worse for which students. The judging process also nudges the student evaluators themselves toward being more thoughtful and discriminating about the different dimensions of teaching and learning. In contrast, ranking merely invites students to record an overall *feeling* with a single number. Students—indeed all evaluators—need to be encouraged to step outside of merely global feelings of approval or disapproval. The most useful and interesting question in evaluation is always "What do you see?"—not "How do you rank it?" As C. S. Lewis (1967) put it, "[P]eople are obviously far more anxious to express their approval and disapproval of things than to describe them" (7).

IQ scores give a vivid illustration of the ranking problem. It is plain that IQ scoring does not represent a commitment to looking carefully at peoples' intelligence—for when we do that, we see different and frequently uncorrelated *kinds* or *dimensions* of intelligence (Gardner 1983). IQ scoring represents, rather, our culture's hunger to rank people along a single scale: a hunger for pecking orders, or, in the military metaphor, for knowing who you can kick and who you have to salute. ("Ten!" mutter the chaps when seeing a beautiful woman.) We see the same principle at work in conventional grading: the use of single numbers on a one-dimensional scale to describe a multidimensional performance, with no stated criteria or categories. Note that I am not arguing against evaluation itself, only against that crude, overly simple way of *representing* evaluation—distorting it, really—into a single unreliable number.[1]

Yet I am not saying we can get rid of *all* single-number, bottom-line, holistic verdicts. For the sake of important decisions, for example, about hiring, promotion, tenure, and merit pay, we often need to make the best estimate we can as to who is an excellent teacher and who is a genuinely poor or irresponsible one. Such decisions can never be wholly trustworthy, but they are not so problematic as fine-grained rankings in the middle range. That is, when we look at answers to the more substantive, judgment-oriented, and analytic student evaluations I have just praised, most teachers will fall somewhere in the middle and get a mixed bag of results: a mixture of strong-, middle-, and weak-rated features and probably many mixed opinions or disagreements among students. But a *few* teachers will get strikingly strong or strikingly weak responses—from many or most students in many or most categories. When we get an unusual degree of agreement this way—and it is supported by other evidence—we are as justified as we can be in reaching a bottom-line holistic verdict that someone is an excellent or poor teacher. But we have no such justification for the fine-grained, holistic, numerical verdicts in the middle.

My point is that we can never have genuine reliability—genuinely trustworthy ranking. But we can get rid of as much untrustworthiness as possible. And since we do not need to give a prize or deny promotion to any of these faculty members in the middle, we don't need to have a bottom-line score for them. What we get instead is a pile of judgment-based responses and an occasion for a conversation between the faculty member and the chair or a committee in order to try to determine what that teacher does well and not so well—and how he or she might teach better.

Just Do It

So how would they work, these official student evaluations of teachers?
I would like to suggest some procedures by way of trying to answer
those common objections or misgivings about student evaluations that
I mentioned at the outset.

*"Students are immature and not yet educated and don't know about
teaching and learning as we do."* It's true that students may not understand what the faculty member has in mind—even her goals and
intentions. But students know more than anyone else about the results
of those intentions and goals. And though students may be mistaken
about their learning—they have been known to lie—they see more of
the teacher than any visitor possibly could. They have more evidence,
more data, for they see lots of *other* teachers in just as much detail, so
they are in an ideal position to make informed comparisons about the
effectiveness of one procedure versus another. Students know more
than most of us about the success of different styles and approaches to
teaching—since we usually see only our own teaching and a tiny bit of
other people's teaching. (It is important here to underline an important
general problem in much evaluation—the "COIK" problem: Clear
Only If Known. Many explanations, lectures, classes, essays, and books
seem admirably clear to evaluators, but only because the evaluators
already understand what is being explained. When the performance is
evaluated by the *intended audience*—who do not already know the
material—a very different verdict often emerges. Notice, for example,
that a hierarchical, deductive, abstract presentation is often just right
for summing up a body of material that you already understand, but it's
just wrong for introducing material that is new and difficult for you to
understand.)

In short, the problem with student evaluators is not whether they
have useful information or knowledge; it is how to *get* their information
or knowledge in a trustworthy form. I turn now to that question.

*"Students just go on feelings, what they like, what's fun or entertaining;
they can be seduced by a good show and easy grades."* There's a blanket
answer to this charge, namely that pleasure and feelings are not so bad.
In the academic world we suffer from a prejudice against what is easy,
popular, and (worst of all student words) "fun." There is no necessary
conflict between something being easy and fun and also producing
good learning. Most people learn better when they enjoy themselves.

But pleasure is not enough. We all know some teachers who are easy
and entertaining but who don't teach so well, and some who are for-
bidding and no fun who, in fact, teach very well. Surely students must

be tempted to rank the former higher than we wish and the latter lower than we wish. (But see Boice 1991 to the contrary, summarizing research which shows that "heavy work loads correlate *positively* with SETs," that is, with favorable student evaluations of teachers.)

In short, a tilt toward easiness can never be completely removed, but it can be substantially diminished to the point where we can put considerable trust in student evaluations of teachers. For the main problem here is *ranking*. We are dumb designers of evaluation unless we ask students lots of questions that have little ranking or evaluative dimension. That is, student judgments, like all judgments, are most valuable when they contain lots of *description*, and least valuable when they give nothing but a number to express a degree of approval or disapproval. We can ask questions like these: "What are the most important things you feel you've learned? What do you see as the most helpful or interesting class or activity? The least helpful or interesting? What do you see as the teacher's major and subsidiary goals or priorities? What were the tests like, and what do you see them as most trying to teach? What were the papers like, and what do you see them as most getting at? Do you see more emphasis placed on information, concepts, skills, or attitudes? How difficult was the work? What side of you did the course and teacher tend to bring out?"

Of course, we will also provide questions that invite rankings, but rankings only about specific criteria or particular dimensions of the course and the teacher's performance—for example, "How would you rate your teacher on knowledge of the subject? Leading discussions? Lecturing? Paper topics? Comments on papers? Choice of readings? Relating with students?"

I am not saying that we should remove all opportunity for holistic verdicts by students about their teachers. Indeed, if we give students an opportunity to say how good or bad they think a teacher was overall— even ask them how much they *liked* or *disliked* the teacher or the course— these feelings are probably less likely to color the students' answers to more particular, substantive questions. Our goal should be to increase the chances that a student who hates a teacher can still go on to acknowledge merit in the teacher's paper assignments or lectures. (Thus, these holistic approval/disapproval questions should perhaps come near the beginning of the form. Also, I believe it helps to ask questions in a form that increases students' self-awareness—e.g., "How did you find yourself reacting to the course content, the assignments, the teacher's style or approach?")

"Student estimations of teachers vary wildly all over the map; their evaluations obviously have no reliability." My response to this charge is to turn the tables and say, "Of course." Surely one of the reasons why faculty so often

distrust student evaluations of teachers is because the disagreement in those evaluations calls too uncomfortably to mind what we accept in published literary criticism but hide in our own grading: namely, the obvious fact that we would get just as much disagreement if we had multiple teachers grading the same student performance. The unreliability of teacher grades is effectively disguised by our handy custom of getting only one opinion.[2]

Some Logistics

It is important to have students actually *write out* all or many of these answers, rather than just check boxes on a computerized form. This gives some intellectual dignity to the evaluation of teachers. But it requires giving the process enough time and attention. The only reason to have a quantified computer system is to reproduce the single-dimensional ranking system that is so obviously flawed (as IQ scores or conventional grades are). There is no need to compare a biology teacher's 2.9 with an English teacher's 2.4. It's not a trustworthy comparison. And even when we must use boxes and numbers because there are so many students, it is important nevertheless to ask all those students to write out answers, too; not just to lend dignity to the process but because the writing will make them more thoughtful when they check boxes.

Since I am suggesting that we collect a pile of qualitative data that a computer cannot reduce to a number, I'm implying that human beings have to look at it and try to reflect on it and, if possible, to discuss what it means. Teachers need discriminating feedback about particular practices and strengths and weaknesses—and we must premise the whole operation on the following crucial principle: *In teaching, as in writing, it is possible to be good in very different ways.* A teacher might be warm or cold, organized or disorganized, easy or hard and still be good.

The logistics of dealing with this data are not really so daunting. Indeed, the very fact of not giving in to ranking or bottom-line verdicts leads naturally to the only kind of system we should trust: one that invokes some human judgment, not just arithmetical calculation. We need a number of very small committees to look at all this data for only a few faculty members each (probably inviting the evaluated teacher also to look at the data and comment). For remember that we don't need this official evaluation system for every teacher every semester. If we ensure that teachers themselves gather informal feedback from students in every course every semester, and get occasional visits from a colleague, this official judging mechanism need only occur every two to three semesters for untenured faculty and every four to five semesters for tenured faculty—not an impossible job. And the point of gathering lots of these student perceptions and not summing them up into a grade is that they would lead to informed discussions of teaching. That's what we need.

I have not talked much about *faculty* evaluation of faculty because that is not my subject in this chapter. But I assume that each evaluation committee would send a member to visit the class of the faculty member in question; that the committee would get examples of the teachers' course material: syllabus, assignments, comments on student writing, and grading (as well as perhaps getting evaluations from a sprinkling of former students). And—very important—the committee would get immeasurable help by seeing a reflective statement by the teacher about her sense of strengths and weaknesses as a teacher and what she sees going on since the last such statement. All of this really constitutes a faculty portfolio.

Looking at this portfolio is not such a difficult task if small committees only have to look at three or four teachers. The committee's job is also easier if members keep in mind the problems of ranking and the value of judging. That is, the committee is not trying to rank teachers with scores, not trying to create precise, bottom-line, numerical *verdicts* of how bad or good the teacher is—except for two important situations: they *do* need to identify very poor teachers and very good ones. But these end-of-spectrum verdicts are not so hard to agree on. The committees' main goal is to analyze and communicate strengths and weaknesses for the vast majority of faculty members who are neither terrible nor extraordinary, so as to help these colleagues teach better.

I'll summarize my main points.

It is impossible to have truly fair, single-number rankings, that is, to get a range of good observers to agree in their verdict about a complex performance. But if we do *less* evaluation, we can do it more carefully and thereby make it a bit more fair. That is, we can avoid the simplification of ranking and use judgment instead—a process of careful looking that discriminates among features or dimensions of a complex performance and is built on the recognition that observers have different priorities. Thus students will be no better than we are at ranking (perhaps worse), but they are good at giving us information for informed judgment: what the teacher did, what they themselves learned, and how they reacted.

We can easily cut down on official, high-stakes, summative evaluation because we can get such good results from more frequent informal, private, low-stakes, formative evaluation. This low-stakes evaluation probably does more to improve teaching than official evaluation does.

Though people are accustomed to ranking almost everything—looking for bottom-line, quantitative verdicts along a single continuum—we seldom actually need these overly simple verdicts. Yes, we need a blunt, holistic verdict when someone's teaching is either genuinely unsatisfactory or exemplary, but most of the time we are better off with more discriminating, multidimensional feedback about the strengths and weaknesses of particular features or practices.

We must find ways to dignify student evaluations of teachers and make the evaluation process thoughtful and reflective rather than mechanical.

Notes

1. In particular, I experienced great relief when I realized that I did not have to grade individual papers just because I had to give grades at the end of the semester. On individual papers, I give feedback about strengths and weaknesses and give general reactions, and stop there, telling students they can come see me starting at midsemester if they want to know how their final grade is shaping up, but not sooner. See Belanoff and Dickson (1991) on portfolios.

2. Someone is bound to object: "How can you say that teachers do not grade reliably in comparison to each other when some students get consistent A's from all their teachers?" Reply: When a student gets all A's, it's not an instance of the same performance getting the same ranking from multiple observers. The straight A student (typically someone who cares a lot about A's and know how to get them) has to make nontrivial adjustments in her performance from teacher to teacher. For the actual performance she gives to one teacher will often enough *not* get her an A from another teacher. Students give good testimony of how often they must make these adjustments from teacher to teacher. We see the same principle if we look at the other side of the coin: talented students who do *not* care about getting A's (and sometimes they are brighter than the typical straight A student) usually get a fair number of B's or even lower grades—the point is that such students *refuse* to adjust their performance from teacher to teacher.

Works Cited

Belanoff, Pat, and Marcia Dickson. 1991. *Portfolios: Process and Product.* Portsmouth, NH: Boynton/Cook.

Boice, Robert. 1991. "Countering Common Misbeliefs about Student Evaluations of Teaching." *Teaching Excellence* (Fall): 1–2. Edited by Marilla Svinicki. Publication of the Professional and Organizational Development Network, University of Nebraska, Lincoln.

Diederich, B. Paul. 1974. *Measuring Growth in English.* Urbana: National Council of Teachers of English.

Elbow, Peter. 1986. "Visiting Pete Sinclair." In *Embracing Contraries: Explorations in Learning and Teaching*, 179–97. New York: Oxford University Press.

Gardner, Howard. 1983. *Frames of Mind: The Theory of Multiple Intelligences*. New York: Basic Books.

Kirschenbaum, Howard, Rodney Napier, and Sidney B. Simon. 1971. *Wad-Ja-Get? The Grading Game in America*. New York: Hart.

Lewis, C. S. 1967. *Studies in Words*. 2nd ed. London: Cambridge University Press.

Smith, Barbara Herrnstein. 1988. *Contingencies of Value: Alternative Perspectives for Critical Theory*. Cambridge, MA: Harvard University Press.

Starch, Daniel, and Edward Elliott. 1913. "Reliability of the Grading of High School Work in English." *School Review* 20: 442–57; "Reliability of Grading Work in Mathematics." *School Review* 21: 254–95; "Reliability of Grading Work in History." *School Review* 21: 676–81. These three are cited and summarized in Kirschenbaum, Napier, and Simon, 258–59.

9 Using Microteaching to Evaluate Teaching Assistants in a Writing Program

Mark A. Baker
Logan High School
Logan, Utah

Joyce A. Kinkead
Utah State University

Like many other university writing programs, the English department at Utah State University relies significantly on teaching assistants. Increasing enrollments (10 percent annually), rising costs, and declining budgets have made the graduate-student-turned-teacher essential for staffing multilevel composition classes. In many ways, these apprentice teachers are boons to a writing program as they bring their enthusiasm, optimism, and energy to the classroom. They often possess a deep desire to teach effectively.

We do realize, though, that such enthusiasm for the teaching role does not necessarily enable a graduate student to evolve quickly into a creative, effective communicator. True, some graduate students enter a program with a wealth of experience in teaching, but others may be amateurs. Even those with experience will most likely be unfamiliar with a particular writing program and will require mentoring. Help in transferring anxious energy into productive teaching skills lies with the writing program administrator (WPA). To aid in channeling that desire to succeed, we have developed a series of activities for our TAs which are incorporated throughout the academic year into their dual roles as instructors and students. And *microteaching* is a key part of this program.

Microteaching Defined

Microteaching is hardly a new concept. It was made popular in the early 1960s and used widely in teacher training. Rather than examining a full class period, in microteaching, novice teachers are asked to analyze a more manageable teaching moment, say only a few minutes, usually recorded on videotape. Most often, this is a *simulated* teaching session.

Microteaching grew out of teacher-training programs in schools of education as a means of preparing future teachers by breaking down a lesson or a set of skills (e.g., effective lecturing, leading class discussion) into discrete parts. It provided not only an opportunity for preservice teachers to practice teaching, but because of its short time frame, many such microteaching lessons could be reviewed by the professor, providing an efficient system for critique. This system came to be rigidly defined and widely used. We present this original concept of microteaching as follows for contrast to the technique we have adopted. Levinson and Menges (1979) recommend formal steps for microteaching which include the following:

1. Teacher is presented with a behaviorally defined teaching skill.
2. Teacher plans a lesson which incorporates the skill and teaches the lesson to a group of approximately five pupils while being videotaped.
3. Teacher receives feedback from peers and supervisors.
4. Teacher reteaches the lesson to another small group, incorporating feedback. (29)

Wilbert McKeachie (1986) describes microteaching as involving the presentation of a lesson

in a brief period; for example, five minutes. The microlesson focuses on the use of a particular skill, such as asking questions, establishing rapport, or eliciting student comments. The microlesson may be videotaped to facilitate review and further practice of the skill desired. (177)

McKeachie goes on to describe microteaching as a form of role-playing (178), for the teacher switches "roles," alternating among researcher, instructor, evaluator, and coach. In this model, the "pupils" may be other preservice teachers (called "microsimulation" by Jensen [1974, 7]) or actual students. In most instances, these are artificial lessons created to fulfill an assignment.

Microteaching Revised

Because we believe in meaningful, purposeful assignments created for real audiences, we chose not to simulate lessons for the camera but to record teaching in actual writing classes. The variety of roles taken on by the TA in the Levinson/Menges model highlights a contrast in our use of microteaching: the TA evaluates his or her own teaching moments; thus, our version of microteaching features self-evaluation. We cannot emphasize this point too strongly. Other WPAs had warned us that teachers of writing often resent the camera eye when they believe it will mean a larger audience scrutinizing the results. Our goal focuses on teachers becoming reflective practitioners, evaluating their teaching, coaching themselves, and discovering classroom strategies and behaviors. (These teachers may invite other viewers of their own accord, however.)

With that comparison of microteaching past and present, let us turn to procedures. During a three-quarter academic year, our TAs videotape a five- to ten-minute portion of a class session each term, review the tape, and write a critique. During the third quarter, they are asked to videotape an "expert" lesson to be placed in the video archives for the following class of TAs; this may be a new session or one already on tape from a previous quarter with which they are particularly pleased. In addition to the videotaping, each TA is observed three times during any quarter by other teachers.

Before we discuss in detail the use of the video camera in helping TAs improve their own pedagogy, a short review of how microteaching fits within our TA program might be helpful for placing this technique in context. In September, before the fall quarter begins, we hold a weeklong workshop for all new TAs. During the workshop, the first half of the ten-week syllabus is discussed, and model lessons from former English 101 classes are demonstrated to the new graduate students by more experienced second-year TAs and lecturers (moving returning TAs from novice to expert status reinforces expectations we hold that TAs grow in independence over the initial year). The video camera silently captures the discourse of practice and reflection for future reference and accustoms the TAs to the idea of a camera being in the classroom. The camera becomes a natural prop, almost invisible to the graduate students.

As the workshop continues, the graduate students role-play both students and teachers, switching back and forth as the situation dictates. The TAs write the initial course assignments so they will have samples for their own classrooms and for the experience of knowing what their students will face. We try out classroom discussion, peer-response groups, and student-teacher conferences, for example, and we review both a student version of the syllabus and a teacher version. The latter syllabus includes textual notes for lectures and ideas for classroom activities which correspond with the student version.

Let us stress that we have master's degree students in our program, no doctoral students, and many of these TAs are not far removed from their own freshman composition classes. Because of this, we begin with a fairly structured approach and syllabus. As a friend of ours once pointed out, "I included religion in my child's upbringing so she would have rules to rebel against." Likewise, we desire some rebellion as the TA matures as a teacher.

Once the fall quarter begins, all first-year TAs meet weekly for two hours in a seminar devoted to the theory and practice of writing, plus continue their professional reading. Our writing program is student-centered in its pedagogy, often an unusual format for TAs who may tend to teach as they were taught (a.k.a. lecture method) if they believe they might lose control of the class. During that time, we review Murray, Elbow, Lindemann, Flower, Moffett, and others and discuss classroom ideas from each TA's personal repertoire. We also continue to model sample lessons from the last half of the syllabus, anticipating and developing them in advance of the assignments. In short, we discuss the needs, questions, frustrations, and victories of each TA's daily teaching experience.

Many of the questions put forth by new TAs arise outside of seminar time, so we must have ready sources of information. To complement this formal interaction, we have developed a mentor program in which second-year TAs observe, coach, and encourage each new TA. To foster this interaction, we have placed both first- and second-year TAs in the same location of departmental offices (an office is assigned to one or two TAs). They share a common hallway, workroom, and lounge, where informal collaboration is constantly in progress. Designated second-year TAs also visit the classroom of each new teaching assistant, observing and coaching through a series of notes centering on "What I See," and "What I Think"—an idea for classroom observation and coaching prompts developed by Jago (1990). Each first-year TA is observed three times quarterly by a mixture of mentors: two second-year TAs (appointed as assistants to the WPA and chosen by their exemplary work during the previous year) and the WPA. By dividing a quarter into three sections, we monitor a TA's development in the first three-week period, the second three-week period, and the final three-week period. The observers share notes with each other. These assistants serve as coaches for the new TA, offering encouragement, looking for trends in teaching behavior, and allowing the new TA to become accustomed to visitors. When the WPA observes the new TA toward the end of the quarter, the fear factor has diminished considerably.

Following each observation, a one-on-one meeting between the mentor and the TA is scheduled as soon as possible. At that time, the TA, as well as the observer, discusses the experience reflected within the "What I See" and "What I Think" format. Common first-year TA concerns include learning to wait longer for responses to questions, incorporating more discussion, relying less on teacher-centered lectures, monitoring body language, using audiovisual equipment, and improving delivery. This entire process of observation and conferences is designed to be as nonthreatening as possible. Joseph Katz notes that "next to the bedroom, the classroom is the most private place in America" (Finkelstein and Smith 1991, 9). We agree. As a result, our intrusions into the "private" domain of each TA are approached gently.

We build a community of teachers by freely discussing in groups what we do in the classroom and why; in many ways, we function as a committee, arguing over philosophy and sharing insights. The evaluation of student essays is done by group, too, using primary-trait scoring. Likewise, the textbook selection (we use common texts) is done by a committee of the whole. Although the seminar is only offered during the fall quarter, the informal sharing in the office hallways, the mentors observing in the classroom, and the primary-trait scoring sessions continue throughout the academic year. The novice TAs are repeatedly exposed to ideas and lessons that work or to experiments as models for risk taking. They are encouraged to steal ideas that have proven successful in other classrooms, putting their own spin on them for ownership. Generally speaking, such strategies do improve a TA's technique. But when reviewing our program, we found that a majority of ideas came from one direction—from the outside. That is, most of the prompting to teach effectively comes from mentors, faculty, and books. Ideas generated from the "tellers" do not always impress the "doers" or make change integral.

Graduate students who teach are invariably caught in a frustrating duality of roles. They are students, yet they want to (and the university expects them to) manage their classes in a professional manner. Year in and year out, fewer than half of our TAs have ever stood in front of the class before, yet we expect such candidates to offer a successful experience for their students and themselves. In examining this paradox, we found that our TAs want help in teaching effectively, but they do not necessarily want to be told how to teach. They long for a certain dependence on the experience of a supervising professor, yet TAs want to feel independent. Our responsibility as mentors includes fostering this independence, helping TAs find ways to evaluate their own performance.

Microteaching in Action

The opportunity for the TAs to guide, nurture, and constructively criticize their own teaching performance is perhaps the strongest advantage of videotaping and reviewing a microteaching unit. The cliché that "the camera never lies" aptly fits here. They expect the camera to tell the truth. They expect the camera to be objective. They expect the camera to offer answers. Armed with such expectations, even the most reluctant of TAs find the camera to be an honest, believable coach. A word of caution, though: TAs tend to invest the video camera with a certain authority, similar to the way first-year writing students view computers as authorities.

Under such circumstances, videotaping is a formative process. When TAs evaluate their individual microteaching units, they cannot help but want to improve their classroom presence—their methods of communication, delivery, and interaction with the students in the classroom. Videotaping and then reviewing a microteaching unit develops within the novice teacher a sense of instructional awareness, for the tape itself gathers a wealth of information. Perhaps for the first time, TAs see their classroom atmosphere from their students' viewpoint, for the camera occupies a seat along with the rest of the students. As a result, the tale captured on celluloid helps the reviewer to determine if the lesson content is appropriate and to what degree the delivery and reception were successful.

Not every coaching technique works for every TA, but in this version of microteaching, TAs retain control of the videotaping process and improvement plan to make it as nonthreatening as possible. Because only five or ten minutes of any class is taped, it plays a minor role, so a TA is not frightened by a full class period of taping. There is plenty to analyze even in this brief timespan, much as a paragraph of a story or a quatrain of a poem yields fertile ground for the literary critic. By repeatedly using microteaching over the course of the academic year, the TAs review their own classroom demeanor and determine the extent of change in delivery or course content. In such a role, the TAs become the summative evaluator of their own teaching behaviors. The video camera may work as a motivator for change when other methods of coaching, peer responding, or student evaluations have failed to encourage certain TAs to improve the dynamics of their classroom

One of our former TAs, Robert, is a typical example of the recalcitrant teacher. Robert refused to believe that he needed to alter his classroom persona even when advised to by several observers—the WPA, one of his TA mentors, or fellow graduate students. He hid behind excuses like

"This observer doesn't care for my style" or "That person didn't understand what I was really doing." Robert did not seriously believe that he actually stood in the corner while he delivered his lectures. As Robert later admitted in his teaching log, in his mind, he was moving about and talking in a dynamic manner. But until he reviewed his taped microteaching unit, he never realized that he actually buried himself in the corner and barely spoke above a whisper. As he noted, "When I see myself, I *see* myself." When no outside influence could, videotaping and self-critique motivated Robert to improve his classroom presence and get out from behind "a smoke-screen alibi of style."

Admittedly, Robert is an unusual, if not extreme, example of an uncoachable TA. Very few graduate students will find solace in the corner. Most graduate students who aspire to teach full-time already possess enough wherewithal to manage competently a class of freshman composition writers. In most cases, videotaping a series of microteaching units serves as an instrument of fine-tuning: Instructors tune up their teaching behavior by periodically visiting the master mechanic—the microteaching process. Upon reviewing a taped lesson, the novice instructor may notice a gap in the delivery, a lack of patience in waiting for student reaction, poor posture, or uncomfortable verbal habits when standing before the class. Each time the formal process is completed, the pedagogy of each TA runs a little bit smoother, a little more professional.

Robert was a traditional graduate student in his early twenties; while nontraditional students often have more experience, they may feel just as ill at ease in the classroom. Laura, a traditional housewife and mother, certainly was uncomfortable in spite of her maturity. Through a series of classroom observations by her mentors, Laura began to realize that she needed some fine-tuning herself, for she had developed a habit of saying "I'm sorry" several times during her mini-lesson deliveries (as often as once per minute). As Laura began to serve as her own formative evaluator through microteaching, she verified for herself what others had noticed. The videotape revealed that, indeed, Laura had developed a habit of repetitively saying "I'm sorry." Her nervousness revealed itself in other ways as well:

> I found myself still not giving enough wait time or even enough time to let them continue their thought process. I noticed that after I got the answer I wanted, I tended to hurry the rest of their response. I also move through the lesson too quickly. I need to take time and be more clear and thorough.

Her microteaching tape made her take notice and offered the proof which pushed her to consciously change undermining habits. Through a series of taped lessons, Laura served as her own personal coach, watching for improvements in her speech patterns. At the end of the year, when she made her summative evaluation, Laura found verification that she had indeed rid herself of that verbal crutch and, in turn, gained self-confidence from that process of fine-tuning. Laura and Robert both improved their classroom performance through self-confrontation via microteaching.

Designing a Self-Evaluation

As WPAs, we are particularly interested in the way TAs analyze their teaching of writing; we care about more than mannerisms, how TAs hold their hands or whether they say "uh" a lot. Donnie wrote in his self-critique, "My microteaching lesson spotlighted audience, but I need, next time, to have more concrete examples, perhaps a quote by a writer on the importance of considering audience." In analyzing their videotapes, TAs need to be aware of surface features as well as content, in addition to noting student behaviors (e.g., engaged, alert, asleep, distracted).

Evaluation guides for viewing a videotaped microteaching lesson exist (see Helling 1981, for instance), but we prefer to have TAs develop their own list of what they consider when evaluating their own teaching. Following is a sample list they developed:

1. Is there class participation in discussion?
2. Is the instructor enthusiastic?
3. Is the instruction clear?
4. Are there transitions?
5. Is the instructor in control?
6. Is the class attentive?
7. Is the lesson worth teaching?
8. What is the applicability of the lesson?
9. What is the instructor's response to class comments/questions?
10. Are there distracting habits or mannerisms?
11. Is the speaking speed too fast or slow?
12. Is there student input and response?
13. How is the lesson organized?
14. Is there a summation of concepts?
15. How well do activities connect to concepts or goals?

These questions may not be as specific as Helling's, for example, "scholarship: indicates sources of knowledge," but we feel that having TAs involved in the structure and organization of microteaching is important. As professionals, we always want to have a say in how we are evaluated.

Microteaching in Other Settings

The classroom is not the only arena that the video camera may enter. Many TAs wish to analyze and improve their individual conferences with students. Upon scrutiny of a videotape, Jane found that she did not practice what she preached:

> I always open the conference by asking what the student would like help on.... I strictly maintain that the paper belongs to the student, and conference time is not a time for me to pick out all the problems and fix them. I took control of the paper in body language, though; I had a tendency to huddle very close and hold the paper a lot.

TAs may want to tape small-group discussion as well; we have had a lot of success with this and with whole-class groups in helping the TA to understand the amount of teacher talk used and how it affects classroom dynamics (e.g., students who do not participate in class discussions may need to be encouraged or questioned directly).

Problems with Microteaching

Taped microteaching is not a pat answer to evaluating TAs, nor is it the absolute coach for self-improvement. For Robert, it was more effective than observation by the WPA, but other TAs prefer human interaction. Sometimes orchestrating the time and machinery necessary to accomplish the task seems more than the apparent worth. And to even begin, there must be equipment, which may not be feasible for a department's operating budget. Finding a camera operator may be a problem (although teachers may ask students, or other TAs, to do this).

TAs acknowledge that having the camera in the classroom can create some pressure and stress. Some of them worry that they cannot get past their appearances (e.g., "My ears are too big!" or "I kept my arms folded") to analyze their teaching. Others fear that the camera does not capture "natural" teaching, that they lose spontaneity when the film is running. Still others simply want to be left alone and see microteaching as a "meaningless hoop" or "one more thing to do."

Although the camera is indeed honest about the teacher, it has difficulty reflecting student behavior as well. The camera records only what is in front of it. Because of its tunnel vision, it may not capture facial expressions or responses.

Advantages to Microteaching

The success of videotaping a microteaching unit depends greatly on the initial introduction of the microteaching idea by the WPA. As mentioned earlier, we place the video camera in the fall workshop—amongst the new TAs—and film each of the microteaching lessons which the mentors demonstrate. During our writing seminar, we offer short demonstrations on the proper use of the camera—extending the tripod, inserting the tape, plus locating the power and record buttons. And our TA handbook (written by TAs) includes printed instructions of the video-making routine. From the very first day that graduate students begin their transformation into classroom teachers, they find themselves in close company with our video camera. Next to the word processor/computer system, the VCR camera is perhaps the most visible, familiar, and widely used piece of electronic machinery.

As TAs finish a yearlong apprenticeship, they evaluate the efficacy of microteaching, and their list of positive comments outnumbers the negative ones. Those who have used microteaching in education classes claim that it is more comfortable to teach in front of real students rather than peers. The pressure is an advantage for some of them because they find that it forces them to be "really prepared" and helps them perform. Watching themselves in the privacy of their own homes on the VCR enables them to look at themselves in different ways: mannerisms, talking too fast, body language, class content. One notes: "It made me aware of pause time to answer questions and helps me ask questions better." They also get a different perspective on students ("Are they attentive?"). It brings home to them the needed improvements. Many cite the permanency of the videotape: "It's a record that can be viewed over and over, while observers' comments are fleeting." Frequently, TAs share their videotapes with each other, even though it is not required. They also invite each other to attend classes, and for those who teach courses simultaneously, the videotape allows them to observe their peers in spite of the conflict in timing. TAs are aware that these videotapes—that is, the ones they want to publish—provide the department and the writing program with a library of materials for future TAs (perhaps a history of writing instruction, too, for research a decade later).

During the heyday of microteaching, several research studies analyzed its effectiveness. Leith (Leith, McNeice, and Fusilier 1989) found that introverts using microteaching benefitted more than extroverts. Our experience with Robert confirms this. Other studies reveal that micro-teaching can be effective in improving actual teaching performance and may help develop student-centered teaching behavior and improve higher-order questioning (Levinson and Menges 1979, 35).

Getting used to being videotaped is another plus, as some of our TAs see videotapes as an excellent way to present themselves for job interviews. As teaching continues to come under scrutiny at the national level (the AAHE Teaching Forum, *Prof Scam*), more and more of the professorial ranks—especially those on tenure track—will find themselves assembling teaching portfolios as outlined by Peter Seldin (1991). One of the suggested items that might be included in the portfolio is a videotape of teaching. A foreign language teacher at Ball State University describes one of the efforts to improve his teaching:

> I had one of my lectures videotaped. I reviewed the tape with the Director of the C[enter for] T[eaching and] L[earning]. . . . This proved to be a valuable experience of self-evaluation which made me more aware of such issues as my style and pace of delivery, physical movement and intonation, as well as the level of clarity in my lecture, amount of repetition and variety in presenting important points, and level of reliance on written notes. (Seldin 1991, 66)

Higher education has traditionally relied primarily on student evaluations as evidence of good teaching, but we all know that a diverse collection of evidence—perhaps including videotapes—is a more reliable indicator of teaching quality.

Things to Remember about Microteaching

Because TAs vary in their learning styles, we try to offer a smorgasbord of evaluative techniques. We do not present microteaching as a cure-all for evaluating TAs but as one of many techniques that might prove useful, depending on the individual TA. We advocate—as does Peter Seldin—a variety of evaluative tools. To conclude, let us summarize some of the concepts we find integral to the successful use of microteaching:

1. Require microteaching over a certain period so that everyone tries this approach, but realize that microteaching is not for everyone; offer a variety of evaluative instruments.

2. Evaluation of microteaching should focus on self-confrontation; WPAs should view microteaching only when invited.

3. Keep an archive of successful lessons that have been "published" by TAs.

4. As WPA, know how to use the equipment and demonstrate it to TAs; have printed instructions available, too.

5. Invite TAs to evaluate microteaching as a technique.

6. TAs should have a voice in the evaluation techniques used.

7. Require teaching or learning logs that include written analysis of the microteaching.

8. As a WPA, practice microteaching yourself.

Works Cited and Consulted

Finkelstein, Martin, and Myrna J. Smith. 1991. *Partners in Learning*. Seton Hall University: New Jersey Institute for Collegiate Teaching and Learning.

Hargie, O.D.W. 1977. "The Effectiveness of Microteaching: A Selective Review." *Educational Review* 29: 87–96.

———. 1978. "Mini-Teaching: An Extension of the Microteaching Format." *British Journal of Teacher Education* 4: 113–18.

Helling, Barbara. 1981. "Looking for Good Teaching: A Guide to Peer Observation." *Innovation Abstracts* 3 (March 6): 7.

Jago, Carol. 1990. "A Journal for Classroom Observations." *CSSEDC Quarterly* 12(3): 5.

Jensen, Richard N. 1974. *Microteaching: Planning and Implementing a Competency-Based Training Program*. Springfield, IL: Thomas.

Leith, William R., Elaine M. McNeice, and Betty B. Fusilier. 1989. *Handbook of Supervision: A Cognitive Behavioral System*. Boston: Little, Brown.

Levinson, Judith L., and Robert J. Menges. 1979. *Improving College Teaching: A Critical Review of Research*. Evanston: Northwestern University Press.

McKeachie, Wilbert J. 1986. *Teaching Tips: A Guidebook for the Beginning College Teacher*. 8th ed. Lexington: D. C. Heath.

Seldin, Peter. 1991. *The Teaching Portfolio: A Practical Guide to Improved Performance and Promotion/Tenure Decisions*. Bolton, MA: Anker.

Smith, A. B. 1974. "A Model Program for Training Teaching Assistants." *Improving College and University Teaching* 22: 198–200.

III Evaluating Specific Faculty Groups

10 Evaluating Adjunct Faculty

David E. Schwalm
Arizona State University West

In this chapter, I will propose a heuristic procedure that should help department chairs or writing program administrators (WPAs) develop reasonable strategies for the evaluation of adjunct faculty, instructors in our programs who have temporary or part-time status. Such an activity is compatible with the Conference on College Composition and Communication's official position on the use of adjunct faculty. While the CCCC statement, originating in the Wyoming Resolution, urges that reliance on adjunct faculty be significantly reduced, it also urges improvement in the working conditions of those who remain. More money or smaller classes are obvious improvements in working conditions, but continuity of employment is also important. If appointment or reappointment of adjunct faculty depends on evaluation, then finding fair and appropriate means of evaluation is an improvement in working conditions. In pursuit of "fair and appropriate means," I will highlight some of the problems involved in the evaluation of adjunct faculty.

There are many forms, foci, and purposes of evaluation. There is no single best way or combination of ways to evaluate adjunct faculty. The basic premise of this chapter is that the evaluation strategies chosen should be suitable to the particular institutional context, which needs to be examined carefully and understood fully. Thus, two heuristics are offered. The first is a series of questions which will help chairs or WPAs to develop a profile of an institution's use of adjunct faculty and the general context in which they are employed. The profile will provide a basis for choosing appropriate evaluation strategies. The second heuristic is a menu of purposes, agents, foci, models, and methods of evaluation from which to choose evaluation strategies.

Adjunct Faculty Profile

Characteristically, a writing program's reliance on adjunct faculty grows in small increments, in reaction to short-term needs rather than as part of a coherent plan. Consequently, answering the following questions may be an informative exercise for chairs or WPAs who have not had occasion to take stock of their use of adjunct faculty. A summary of the answers to these questions (and any additional questions they might suggest) will provide indispensable information for determining how adjunct faculty should be evaluated.

1. How many adjunct faculty does your department employ?
2. What are the minimum qualifications for adjunct faculty?
3. When you have more applicants than positions, according to what criteria do you rank applicants?
4. What courses do adjunct faculty teach in your department?
5. Describe as fully as possible the physical working conditions of adjunct faculty (office space, support staff, office machines, access to computers, copying or duplicating, etc.).
6. How much input do adjunct faculty have into the content of the courses they teach (standard syllabus, prescribed textbooks, etc.)?
7. How much are your adjunct faculty paid? Do they get benefits?
8. Are your adjunct faculty appointed semester by semester, annually, longer contracts (note such matters as a drop-in adjunct faculty hiring in the spring semester)?
9. How far in advance of the start of the semester are your adjunct faculty hired?
10. What is the maximum number of courses adjunct faculty can teach each semester? What is a typical teaching load?
11. What percentage of your adjunct faculty teach at more than one place?
12. What percentage of your adjunct faculty are minorities? Women?
13. How do you evaluate the teaching of tenured and tenure-track faculty members in your department?
14. How do you evaluate the teaching of graduate assistants in your department?

The following paragraph exemplifies an adjunct faculty profile summary for the English department at a large public university:

We typically employ 25–30 adjunct faculty (here called faculty associates or FAs) each semester, drawing from a qualified pool of about 40–50. The minimum requirement for employment is an M.A. (not necessarily in English) or M.F.A., but we look for teaching experience as well. Many of our FAs were formerly our own teaching assistants. For reappointment we use a point system that values seniority heavily, then level of degree, then teaching evaluations. The system favors incumbents, although new applicants with special abilities (e.g., knowledge of ESL or technical writing) can "jump the line." Our FAs are teaching 98 courses this semester—83 composition courses and 15 other courses. They are teaching 42 percent of all the composition courses offered this semester. Right now, all FAs have their own desks and mailboxes but share offices with from 2 to 15 others. They have access to support services, a computer lab, common telephone with limited calling range, telephone message services, limited xeroxing, generous dittoing, etc. They are paid $1,600–$1,800 per course, depending on degree and seniority. Those who teach three or more courses get benefits. Some are on yearly contracts; others are on semester contracts—a distinction largely determined by seniority. Most are hired well in advance of the beginning of the semester, but some are hired at the last minute. All hirings are contingent upon need and funding, and in most cases the actual number of courses offered will change at the last minute. FAs can teach a maximum of five courses; they teach an average of four. Approximately 30 percent also teach one or more courses at the community college or at proprietary colleges. Sixty percent are women. Two percent are minorities. Most, but not all, make their living as FAs. In the composition courses that constitute most of their teaching, FAs are given a standard syllabus and a limited choice of textbooks. They have some leeway in implementing the syllabus and in choosing writing assignments. The teaching of tenure/tenure-track faculty in the department is evaluated only by a required, self-administered "student attitude" questionnaire. The teaching of TAs is evaluated by multiple measures: student attitude questionnaire, competency questionnaire, faculty class visits, review of graded papers, review of grade distributions, multiple class visits by peers.

Chairs and WPAs who have completed the adjunct faculty-use profile should then turn to the following menu of evaluation options to determine which options are compatible with the working conditions of adjunct faculty.

Evaluation Options

1. Purposes of Evaluation:
   a. Formative Emphasis;
   b. Summative Emphasis.

This choice sets the context for all subsequent choices. Formative evaluation of teaching is done primarily for the benefit of the instructor being evaluated. It provides feedback to help the instructor become a better teacher. It is not done to determine who will be rehired, who will get pay raises, or who will get the teaching award. These are the province of summative evaluation of teaching, a kind of evaluation concerned primarily with accountability and comparative excellence. Summative evaluation is useful for making general claims about the quality of teaching in a program or department or, more negatively, for protecting students from incompetent instructors. Thus, summative evaluation may emphasize identifying either *competence* (Does the instructor successfully fulfill the basic obligations of the job?) or *excellence* (To what extent does the instructor exceed these basic obligations?). These two objectives require the asking of rather different questions, how ever they are asked. Generally, the audience for summative evaluation is not primarily the person being evaluated.

Perhaps all teaching evaluation ought to be formative, and it probably is, to some extent. But an emphasis on formative evaluation is an absolute necessity in situations where an institution is highly dependent upon a very limited pool of adjunct faculty, where the quality of instruction depends upon improving the skills of the few qualified teachers available, a common situation in rural areas and small towns. On the other hand, institutions in large urban areas often have an embarrassment of riches in their adjunct faculty pool and need not be much concerned about faculty development (although the ethical implications of such practices are alarming). The competitive situation may almost force an emphasis on summative evaluation as a means of equitably deciding who gets hired and retained.

2. Focus of Evaluation:
   a. Teaching;
   b. Professional Activity;
   c. Institutional Service.

These are the three common foci for tenure-track faculty evaluation. Teaching includes such things as classroom performance, grading, development of teaching materials and course syllabi, supervision of graduate theses, and so on. Professional activity usually includes such matters as publication, presentations at conferences, and professional development activities such as workshops, classes, seminars, conferences, etc. Institutional service includes work on department, college, or university committees as well as service in professional organizations and even community groups.

Just which of these foci are appropriate for adjunct faculty evaluation depends upon what can reasonably and fairly be expected of adjuncts in a given situation. Adjunct faculty teaching five or more courses distributed over more than one institution cannot reasonably be evaluated on their scholarly productivity or their institutional service. Yet at institutions that encourage professional development for adjuncts, providing workshops or money to travel to conferences, it is reasonable to reward adjunct faculty who take advantage of these opportunities. Adjunct faculty who do not have much input into curriculum cannot reasonably be evaluated on their teaching materials and syllabi, whereas these materials would be critical to evaluation when adjunct faculty design their own courses and choose their own textbooks.

3. Model for Evaluation:
    a. Tenure-Track Faculty Model;
    b. Graduate Assistant Model;
    c. Adjunct Faculty Model.

Most departments can choose whether to evaluate adjunct faculty in the same way tenured/tenure-track faculty are evaluated, in the same way graduate teaching assistants are evaluated, or in yet another way altogether. This choice indicates how adjunct faculty are viewed in the department. This is often not a problem in departments where nobody receives much evaluation or everyone is evaluated by multiple measures. The reality is that at most large universities, like the university profiled above, TAs are heavily evaluated while tenured/tenure-track faculty are hardly evaluated at all. Development of a model of evaluation for adjunct faculty then becomes a political tightrope act, central to defining the status of adjuncts in the department.

4. Evaluation Agents:
    a. Self-Evaluation;
    b. Evaluation by Students;
    c. Evaluation by Peers;
    d. Evaluation by Supervisors.

It is generally desirable to have input from all four sources, whether the primary purpose is formative or summative. With regard to adjunct faculty, self-evaluation and student evaluation are currently conventional practices. Evaluation by peers raises interesting political questions: Who is an adjunct faculty member's peer? To suggest that the tenured/tenure-track faculty and adjunct faculty are peers is a generous political statement that will, nonetheless, be greeted with derision on payday. Obvious conflict-of-interest problems arise if adjunct faculty evaluate each other in a situation where summative evaluation affects reappointment and many adjunct faculty are competing with one another for a limited number of jobs. (This situation could skew the reliability of self-evaluation as well). Some institutions mix TAs and adjunct faculty as peers, an equation not often viewed positively by adjunct faculty (even though TAs in Ph.D. programs may have higher qualifications and more experience than some adjunct faculty). Evaluation by supervisors may include evaluation by full-time faculty, by the WPA, the department chair, or the dean, or any combination of these. The choice of evaluation agent makes a statement about the professional status of adjunct faculty in the department.

5. Method of Evaluating Teaching:
   a. Student Questionnaire;
   b. Class Visit(s);
   c. Review of Teaching Materials;
   d. Self-Report;
   e. Review of Graded Papers;
   f. Videotape;
   g. Student Outcomes (performance);
   h. Teaching Portfolio.

The conventional wisdom in teaching evaluation is that only multiple measures will yield valid and reliable evaluation of teaching. If so, then multiple measures really must be used for summative evaluation, since reappointment, raises, or both may be at stake. But the measures suggested above individually and collectively pose enormous problems. Will the student questionnaire attempt to identify whether the instructor did an excellent job or a competent job? How many class visits are necessary to provide a valid assessment? Who will do them? Is there any point in reviewing teaching materials if the adjunct faculty teach a standard syllabus? By what standards are teaching materials to be judged? Are self-reports likely to be informative if adjuncts are in the position of competing for a limited number of positions? Is there a uniform standard by which paper grading can be judged? Who will take the videotapes, and who will review them? How will student outcomes be measured (grades are generally not acceptable for other assessment purposes)?

Summative evaluation using multiple measures can be a real problem in departments using large numbers of adjunct faculty. Someone has to review all of these materials. While this may be possible in a department that employs two or three adjunct faculty, it becomes a logistical nightmare in a department that employs twenty or thirty adjuncts. Although evaluation this thorough is not common, some departments do require such materials from new tenure-track faculty every year or so and from tenured faculty less often. Even the largest departments will have only a few assistant professors to evaluate in this manner, and the task of reviewing is taken seriously because tenure is at stake. Those same departments might have thirty or more adjunct faculty (in addition to eighty to one hundred TAs whose teaching must be evaluated, too). Under these circumstances, evaluation of the teaching of adjunct faculty could become a major departmental service responsibility.

Were adjunct evaluation to be formative only, however, many of the logistical problems of using multiple measures would disappear. The adjunct faculty member is the only person obliged to review all of the materials; the very act of putting together a teaching portfolio would be formative.

Applying the Heuristics

I will conclude by examining the evaluation options in terms of the profile of adjunct faculty use included above.

1. Purposes of Evaluation.

Because this department has a competitive adjunct faculty pool, it could simply opt for some sort of summative evaluation strategy to protect students from poor instruction and eschew any responsibility for faculty development. However, in order to get some staffing stability and continuity, the department has chosen to emphasize seniority and thereby to privilege incumbency; new adjunct faculty are hired because they have special abilities, because of increased need, or because someone left—and only occasionally because someone was not reappointed. A person with an M.A. will not be dismissed because someone with a Ph.D. comes along. Thus, this department, consciously or unconsciously, has set up a situation that favors an emphasis on formative assessment, even though some summative assessment is necessary to insure competent instruction.

2. Focus of Evaluation.

The fact that the typical course load is four courses, with some adjuncts teaching five and 30 percent teaching additional courses elsewhere, indicates that teaching alone should be the focus of evaluation. Given the low pay scale, combined with heavy teaching loads, it would be unreasonable to expect or require institutional service or much by way of professional activity. Adjunct faculty are clearly hired to teach. Evidence about service or professional activity (especially related to teaching) could certainly be considered but could not fairly be sought or expected.

3. Model for Evaluation.

The teaching of the tenure-track faculty in this department is evaluated only by self-administered, student-attitude questionnaires in each class every semester. The graduate teaching assistants are more intensively evaluated, with multiple measures emphasizing formative evaluation. The adjunct faculty currently are evaluated in the same way the faculty are, although if they are teaching composition classes, they must administer the competency questionnaire the TAs use. The WPA has chosen to treat the TAs and the adjunct faculty as distinct groups and wishes to maintain that distinction in developing a teaching-evaluation model but is not confident that adjunct faculty or their students are well served by the faculty model—which is barely any evaluation at all, formative or summative.

4. Evaluation Agents.

Adjunct faculty are already evaluated by their students. Formalized self-evaluation would impose a bit of extra work, but the process itself might be salutary. The product might take the form of a teaching portfolio which could be reviewed by a supervisor. Because of the teaching loads, it would be unreasonable and logistically impossible to require adjunct faculty to review one another, especially if the review included class visits. The tenured/tenure-track faculty already somewhat reluctantly visit the classes of eighty to ninety TAs and would not welcome the additional responsibility of visiting thirty adjunct faculty. It is doubtful that anything useful would come of class visits conducted by resentful faculty. In this department, students, adjunct faculty themselves, and supervisors (the chair or WPA) are the most eligible evaluation agents.

5. Method of Evaluating Teaching.

Adjunct faculty in the department currently administer two student questionnaires—one of which attempts to identify excellence in classroom performance and a second that attempts to check to see if the instructor is meeting the basic obligations of the job—meeting classes, grading papers, and so on (see figure 1). Both of these are basically summative, not providing much useful information to the instructor. The questionnaires do indicate to the department whether or not the instructor is competent. The department's decision to value seniority and thus to favor incumbency suggests that some additional formative evaluation of teaching is necessary. Conditions in the department preclude any type of evaluation that would require excessive amounts of time from the tenured/tenure-track faculty (visiting classes, reviewing

INSTRUCTOR EVALUATION—FIRST-YEAR COMPOSITION

Instructor's Name: Grade you expect in course:

Instructions: Circle the most accurate response to each item, below.

1. Your writing has improved as a result of taking this course.

   Yes   No

2. You were provided with a written syllabus showing the schedule of assignments for the semester.

   Yes   No

3. You were given written course guidelines explaining the instructor's policies on such matters as late papers, attendance, grading procedures, etc.

   Yes   No

4. The instructor held all scheduled class meetings.

   Yes   No (If "no," how many classes were cancelled?_____)

5. The instructor was available outside of class during office hours or by appointment.

   Yes   No

6. The instructor met the class for the full period.

   always   usually   sometimes   rarely   never

7. Paper assignments were presented clearly, either orally or in writing.

   always   usually   sometimes   rarely   never

8. You were asked to submit rough drafts of formal papers and to revise these rough drafts after receiving comments on them from the instructor and/or classmates.

   always   usually   sometimes   rarely   never

9. The instructor marked and returned papers or rough drafts promptly (i.e., within a week or before next draft or paper was due).

   always   usually   sometimes   rarely   never

10. The comments you received on rough drafts were helpful to you in revising.

    always   usually   sometimes   rarely   never

11. You understood why you got the grades you did on papers and other assignments.

    always   usually   sometimes   rarely   never

Fig. 1. Student questionnaire.

videos or sets of graded papers), and the teaching loads of the adjunct faculty preclude any kind of systematic peer evaluation. Thus it would seem that the student questionnaires could best be supplemented by self-report, possibly in the form of a teaching portfolio. Without being terribly time-consuming, assembling and commenting on the portfolio would be beneficial for the adjunct faculty member, and the portfolios could be reviewed briefly by the WPA or department chair (mainly to ensure compliance). The addition of the portfolio would create a better balance between summative and formative assessment than currently exists in the department.

The role of adjunct faculty in a program or department often increases incrementally, without conscious planning and without much aware-ness of its magnitude. The use of the first of these two heuristics will encourage department administrators to take a close look at their use of adjunct faculty to determine what their role is or should be. The use of the menu of evaluation strategies offered by the second heuristic in the context of the adjunct faculty profile may also make department admin-istrators aware of the extent to which the method of evaluation defines the status of adjuncts in the department and sends messages, intended or not, about departmental attitudes toward part-time faculty. The combined use of these two heuristics can help department chairs or WPAs devise ways of evaluating adjunct faculty that are both reasoned and reasonable in the context of the program and will benefit both the program and the adjunct faculty.

11 Teaching Assistants as Collaborators in Their Preparation and Evaluation

Irwin Weiser
Purdue University

The literature on the evaluation of teachers distinguishes between two purposes evaluation may serve: evaluation for personnel decisions such as promotion and retention and evaluation for improving instructors' effectiveness. While in practice these purposes are not always discrete, this distinction is helpful to those responsible for determining when and by what means instructors are to be evaluated. More importantly, programs which assume that the purpose of evaluating writing teachers is to enable them to become more effective may take a broader view of how evaluation fits into their programs, expanding the notion of evaluation to include evaluation by the writing teachers of the preparation they receive and giving them a role in the planning of that preparation. It is this broad view of evaluation that I wish to focus on in this discussion. By describing the development and function of several questionnaires used in the planning of our orientation program, the seminar in teaching composition that new teaching assistants are required to take, and the composition class itself, I hope to show that involving new writing teachers in their preparation contributes to their success in meeting the goals of the program.

Specifically, I will discuss a survey sent to all new teaching assistants following their appointment which they complete and return prior to their week-long orientation, an evaluation of the mentoring they receive in the teaching practicum during their first year as instructors in freshman composition, and the instructor evaluation questionnaire students complete toward the end of their required composition courses. The questionnaires are reproduced in figures 1–3.

Preorientation Survey

The motive for developing this survey (figure 1) grew from my concern that our orientation program operated in something of a vacuum. That

NEW TEACHING ASSISTANT SURVEY

By taking a few minutes to answer the following questions, you can help tailor this year's orientation program for new teaching assistants to your concerns and interests.

PART I: Background and Experience

1. Have you taught composition previously?

   Yes _____   No _____

2. If your answer to 1 is "yes", how many composition courses have you taught?

   1–3 _____   4–6 _____   7–10 _____   Over 10 _____

3. Have you had other kinds of college teaching experience? If so, specify the kinds of teaching you have done.

4. Have you had elementary, middle, or high school teaching experience?

   Yes _____   No _____

5. Have you had any formal (i.e., classes) or informal (i.e., workshops, inservice programs) training in teaching writing?

   Yes _____   No _____

   If you answer "yes", please describe your training briefly. Use the back of this page if you need more space.

6. Have you taken an introductory composition course yourself?

   Yes _____   No _____

   If you answer "yes", please describe briefly the course (length of course, approximate number of papers, required reading, etc.). Use the back of this page if you wish.

   If you answer "no", but such a course was generally required, did you test out, were you exempted, or did you fulfill the requirement in some other way (by taking a more advanced course, for example)?

7. Which best describes the type of undergraduate school you attended?

   _____ American, publicly supported, over 10,000 students
   _____ American, publicly supported, under 10,000 students
   _____ American, privately supported, over 10,000 students
   _____ American, privately supported, under 10,000 students
   _____ College or university not in United States

PART II: Subjects of Interest to You

Please indicate your interest in discussing and learning about each of the following by numerically ranking the items in each group. Use 1 to indicate the item most important to you in each group, 2 for the next most important, and so on.

Fig 1. Preorientation survey.

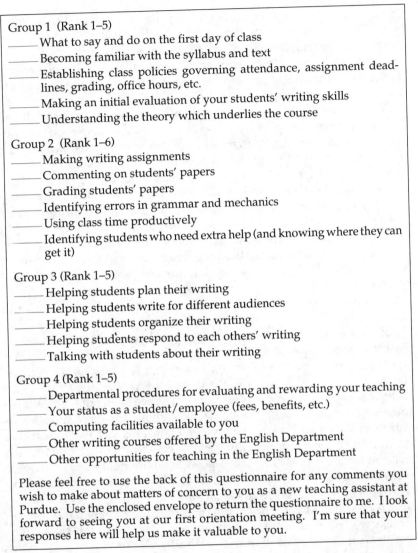

Group 1 (Rank 1–5)
_____ What to say and do on the first day of class
_____ Becoming familiar with the syllabus and text
_____ Establishing class policies governing attendance, assignment deadlines, grading, office hours, etc.
_____ Making an initial evaluation of your students' writing skills
_____ Understanding the theory which underlies the course

Group 2 (Rank 1–6)
_____ Making writing assignments
_____ Commenting on students' papers
_____ Grading students' papers
_____ Identifying errors in grammar and mechanics
_____ Using class time productively
_____ Identifying students who need extra help (and knowing where they can get it)

Group 3 (Rank 1–5)
_____ Helping students plan their writing
_____ Helping students write for different audiences
_____ Helping students organize their writing
_____ Helping students respond to each others' writing
_____ Talking with students about their writing

Group 4 (Rank 1–5)
_____ Departmental procedures for evaluating and rewarding your teaching
_____ Your status as a student/employee (fees, benefits, etc.)
_____ Computing facilities available to you
_____ Other writing courses offered by the English Department
_____ Other opportunities for teaching in the English Department

Please feel free to use the back of this questionnaire for any comments you wish to make about matters of concern to you as a new teaching assistant at Purdue. Use the enclosed envelope to return the questionnaire to me. I look forward to seeing you at our first orientation meeting. I'm sure that your responses here will help us make it valuable to you.

Fig. 1. *Continued.*

is, we knew what we thought new teachers of writing should know, both about the effective teaching of writing and about the nuts and bolts of their new institutional home, but we had no assurance that what we were providing coincided with what the teaching assistants felt they needed to know in order to be ready to begin teaching the following week. I worried that such a difference in expectations would diminish the effectiveness of our orientation since the unarticulated concerns of new teaching assistants might prevent them from absorbing the information and instruction we provide them. The survey is designed to give those of us who participate in the orientation and mentoring of teaching assistants some insight into the background, priorities, and concerns of each year's new group.

The survey elicits several kinds of information (for a more detailed analysis of typical responses, see Weiser 1990). Part I focuses on the prior educational and teaching experience of the respondents, providing a basic profile of the group. Part II asks the TAs to rank four groups of items concerning teaching writing. Group 1 contains five items which I think should be of fairly immediate concern to new teachers since they involve getting started in the class. Group 2 asks TAs to rank some activities integral to (or traditionally considered integral to) teaching writing. Group 3 deliberately asks about rhetorical and pedagogical techniques which are part of teaching writing as a process and as a social act, two theoretical positions which guide our program. These items, I suspect, are consciousness raising since their very presence brings them to the attention of the teaching assistants and implies their relevance to the teaching of writing.

Since we began using this survey several years ago, the responses have led to a number of changes in the structure of our orientation and mentoring programs. Because, for example, most new teaching assistants show a strong interest in the theory underlying the course, I include a theoretical introduction in the talk I give on the first morning of orientation, emphasizing the similarities among the three specific syllabi used in the small practicum (or mentor) groups each will be working in during the year. In addition, I look carefully at questions which receive responses that indicate a need for more deliberate consciousness-raising efforts. For example, last year's respondents ranked audience concerns relatively low, so I included in my early talk a discussion of the centrality of audience to the rhetorical situation and the ways in which we try to encourage audience awareness through the assignments we make. However, because of the diversity of responses to many of the questions, we have, over the past three years, eliminated many of the large-group sessions on particular aspects of teaching writing and instead have many more opportunities for new teaching assistants to meet in their mentor groups, where specific considerations of syllabi, class activities, and teaching strategies can take place more easily, and where, because the groups are small and informal, it is not as intimidating for them to ask questions.

The survey has consistently revealed differences between experienced and inexperienced teaching assistants, which led us to change the way we assign students to their mentor groups for the year. In the past, experienced and inexperienced teachers were deliberately placed together in mentor groups under the assumption that the new teachers, in particular, could learn from the more experienced ones. While this assumption still makes sense, the survey responses have shown enough differences to warrant forming one or more groups made up of people who have had prior training and teaching experience in composition. These teaching assistants no longer find themselves covering material which is familiar to them. More interestingly, we have been able to try some new approaches to teaching with the experienced TAs since they are already familiar with the theoretical and practical matters of teaching a process-oriented composition class. And while the inexperienced teaching assistants may be missing some of the benefits of having experienced teachers in their mentor group, there appears to be something of a "we're all in the same boat" effect within groups of novices. In the groups of inexperienced teachers I have worked with over the past two years, I have detected none of the impatience I had sometimes witnessed when people new to the classroom asked questions which the experienced teachers did not need to spend time on. There also appears to be more willingness to figure out how to deal with problems within the group, perhaps because they do not feel that someone else already has the answer. From the mentors' perspective, having groups which are similar in experience makes it easier to arrange sessions which will benefit everyone.

As a mentor and as a program director, I have found that this survey provides me with information about new teaching assistants which enables me to plan practicum and orientation programs that are responsive to their concerns. Doing so ultimately plays a role in the evaluation of these teachers since their training is designed around issues important to their own sense of success. Further, as I will discuss in more detail later, the survey contributes to their sense of participation in a community which values them and which wants them to succeed.

Evaluations of Mentors

The central element of our preparation of teaching assistants is the mentoring program. Groups of five to eight new teaching assistants meet during orientation week and then weekly during their first year with a faculty member or experienced senior teaching assistant to discuss both the theory and practice of teaching composition. Officially, participation in a mentor group means taking a one-credit-per-semester

Practicum in the Teaching of College Composition (similar courses and mentor groups are in place for other writing courses taught by teaching assistants). In addition to planning the practicum meetings, mentors observe classes several times each semester, review papers people in their groups have commented on and/or graded, and write an evaluation (figure 2) of the performance of each teaching assistant in the group each semester. Copies of these evaluations are given to both the teaching assistant and the director of composition.

But it is not these evaluations, typical of most teacher-preparation programs, I wish to discuss. Indeed, because mentors and teaching assistants have a great deal of contact, these formal evaluations primarily function as records of what the mentor and teaching assistant have already discussed following class visits or the review of papers. Instead, I want to describe the evaluation of and for their mentors that teaching assistants complete each semester.

As is the case with the preorientation survey, this evaluation enables teaching assistants to participate in their own preparation through their comments about the amount and kind of support they are receiving from their mentors. The anonymous questionnaires are submitted first to the director of composition, and then given to the mentors at the end of each semester. Though at the end of the first semester teaching assistants may be reluctant to criticize their mentor—knowing that they will spend another semester with him or her—this midyear evaluation is important because it allows the mentor to make changes that address the concerns of the teaching assistants in the group.

Like the questions in the preorientation survey, and like those in the instructor evaluation questionnaire to be described later, the questions used for mentor evaluation are designed to suggest what the respondents should be experiencing—in this case, what mentoring should be accomplishing, as we have developed it in our program. This is particularly true of those questions which ask "How well do . . ." or "How have . . . ," which imply that mentor-group sessions should be addressing immediate concerns for teaching specific material, should address positive interaction with students, should address evaluation and grading, and that mentors should follow up observations of teaching with discussions, and so on. Other questions, numbers 13 through 15, invite more general commentary on changes teaching assistants would like to see in the mentor group.

The responses to these evaluation questions have generally been quite positive, indicating to me and to the other mentors that our program is indeed providing teaching assistants with the kind of support that they desire and that we want them to receive. The typical response includes a lot of praise for the mentor—sometimes in single-word comments like "Absolutely!" and sometimes in great detail, such as references to specific problems of classroom discipline or absenteeism about which the mentor advised the teaching assistant. After reading these evaluations for several years, one of the clearest generalizations I can draw is that classroom observations, despite the amount of anxiety they cause, and the follow-up discussions of the observations are considered by the teaching assistants to be the most valuable component of the mentoring program. New teaching assistants have also consistently indicated the value of sample student writing, workshop activities, and similar supplements their mentors provide them, and of the time spent working on evaluation of student writing. Criticisms have been fairly minor. Last year, an overcommitted mentor was gently chastised by his mentor group for often switching the weekly meeting time during the first semester. According to the mentor, the teaching assistants had not indicated during the semester that this was a problem for them, but reading it on the evaluation enabled him to address it both by apologizing for inconveniencing them and by being sure he scheduled the second-semester meetings at a time he would always have free. Sometimes more experienced teaching assistants have felt that their mentor did not allow them enough flexibility to modify the course, especially during their first semester. This response is not surprising, given that some of our "new" teaching assistants have taught composition for several years before beginning their work here, but neither is it particularly troublesome since we are aware—and we try to emphasize this to the teaching assistants—that the composing theories and pedagogical approaches which guide our courses may differ from those with which they are familiar. By the second-semester evaluation, teaching assistants usually respond more positively to this question, reflecting, I believe, both our intentional encouragement of experimentation and their own increased understanding of the approaches we support.

Beyond what the specific responses tell us about how well the mentoring program addresses the concerns of the teaching assistants, this evaluation, like the preorientation questionnaire, makes teaching assistants collaborators in their preparation. By soliciting the opinions of new teaching assistants, we include them immediately and continually in the community of teachers our writing program wants to foster.

Student Evaluation of Composition Instruction

This final element of evaluation in our composition program is what most educators and students typically think of first when they consider

MENTOR EVALUATION QUESTIONS
FOR FRESHMAN COMPOSITION

Please respond to each of the following questions as fully and specifically as you can. Feel free to include additional comments about mentoring after you have responded to the questions.

1. How well do mentor-group meetings address your immediate concerns for teaching specific material for the course?

2. How well do mentor-group meetings address general and/or theoretical issues of teaching writing (or complement such discussion in courses you take)? How effectively is the relationship between these issues and classroom teaching articulated?

3. How well do mentor-group meetings cover material which helps you teach more confidently and effectively?

4. How well do mentor-group meetings or conferences with your mentor address positive interaction with and motivation of students?

5. How well do mentor-group meetings or conferences with your mentor address practical concerns of classroom management, handling difficult students, dealing with chronic absenteeism, etc.?

6. How well do mentor-group meetings address evaluation and grading?

7. If your mentor provides you with supplementary teaching materials, e.g., sample student papers, appropriate exercises, workshops, etc.,
   a. which materials have been helpful to you?
   b. how have those materials been helpful?
   c. were there assignments for which you needed additional materials?

8. If your mentor assigns readings in composition theory and practice, do the readings help you:
   a. teach more effectively?
   b. understand theories or issues which address the complexity of teaching writing?

9. To what extent has your mentor introduced a variety of teaching methods and/or strategies (e.g., collaborative workshops, conferencing) and advised you about how and when to incorporate them?

10. How have your mentor's observations of your teaching and follow-up discussions helped you recognize your strengths and weaknesses as a teacher?

11. How have your mentor's comments about your response to and grading of student writing helped you become a better and/or more confident evaluator of your students' work?

12. Is your mentor responsive to specific adaptations and flexibility within the structure of the course which help you address the specific needs of your individual classes?

Fig. 2. Mentor evaluation questionnaire.

13. Are there aspects of your mentoring which you feel should receive more attention?

14. Are there aspects of your mentoring which you feel should receive less attention or be omitted?

15. What changes in mentoring would you like your mentor to implement for next semester?

16. Do you feel that the mentoring process is preparing you to be a confident, knowledgeable, more independent teacher of freshman composition?

Fig. 2. *Continued.*

evaluating teachers. The end-of-term evaluation by students of their instructors has an established place in higher education, and despite whatever our personal opinions of such evaluations might be, research has shown that student evaluation is both reliable and valid if the instrument is appropriately designed and appropriately interpreted (see Seldin 1980, and Braskamp, Brandenburg, and Ory 1984 for summaries of research).

Our evaluation questionnaire (figure 3) has evolved over the past several years, its evolution prompted by the recognition of the department's composition committee that neither the universitywide cafeteria system questionnaire, despite its 200+ questions to choose from, nor the more brief, yet nevertheless generic, departmental form was appropriate for evaluating the teaching of introductory composition. Neither form allowed instructors or anyone else looking at it to determine whether students believed that the specific goals of the writing program were being met; neither allowed instructors to tailor the evaluation questions to reflect particular pedagogical approaches or intellectual emphases. Questions on both forms tended to be of the type Weimer (1990) has identified as global, rather than departmental, programmatic, or individual.

Currently, our questionnaire contains forty-two items, nearly equally divided between questions which focus primarily on the course and questions which focus on the instructor. The initial questions were developed by the department's composition committee, but in keeping with our goal of including teaching assistants in their preparation and evaluation, there is an open invitation for instructors to request the addition of new questions. In the version which appears in figure 3, items 32, 35, 36, and 38 represent additions recommended by teaching assistants. Recently, an instructor who has been using a cultural studies approach and working with other teaching assistants as they learn to do so, too, has suggested the addition of several new questions such as

COMPOSITION PROGRAM STUDENT EVALUATION
ITEM SELECTION CATALOG

1. This course helped me become a better writer.
2. This course helped me plan my writing.
3. This course helped me state a main idea (thesis, focus).
4. This course helped me support a main idea (thesis, focus).
5. This course helped me organize my ideas and information.
6. This course helped me adjust my writing to the needs of readers.
7. This course helped me adjust my word choice to my writing purpose.
8. This course helped me adjust my sentences to my writing purpose.
9. This course helped me revise my papers.
10. This course helped me edit my papers to correct errors.
11. This course helped me analyze my own and other students' writing.
12. This course helped me clarify my ideas through writing.
13. This course helped me write in other courses.
14. This course helped me develop a research question or problem.
15. This course helped me find information in the library.
16. This course helped me evaluate what I read.
17. This course helped me synthesize information from several sources.
18. This course helped me support a main idea through research.
19. This course helped me document sources.
20. My teacher regularly prepares for class.
21. My teacher presents information clearly and effectively.
22. My teacher encourages questions and class discussions.
23. My teacher relates reading assignments to writing assignments.
24. My teacher uses class time productively.
25. My teacher encourages group work for writing.
26. My teacher relates assignments to the goals of the course.
27. My teacher explains the purpose of writing assignments.
28. My teacher explains standards for grading.
29. My teacher returns most assignments within a week.
30. Comments on my papers help me improve my writing.
31. My teacher encourages students to use the Writing Lab.
32. My teacher is available to confer outside of class.
33. Conferences with my teacher have been valuable to me.
34. My teacher responds to questions with consideration.
35. My teacher is interested in me as a person as well as a student.
36. My teacher is friendly and accessible.
37. My teacher explains policies for attendance and late assignments.
38. My teacher shows cultural awareness and sensitivity to students.

Fig. 3. Instructor evaluation questionnaire.

901. My teacher motivates me to do my best work.
902. My instructor explains difficult material clearly.
903. Course assignments are interesting and stimulating.
904. Overall, this course is among the best I have ever taken.

Fig. 3. *Continued.*

"This course helped me understand the ways in which cultural issues affect academic knowledge," and "This course introduced me to new ways of interpreting my academic and social experiences." The ability of instructors to add questions like these enables them to develop evaluation questionnaires which are consistent with their pedagogical practices and to learn whether their students believe that those practices are successful.

Because our evaluation forms are prepared and summarized by the university's Center for Instructional Services in the same format as the more general cafeteria system survey, the four university core questions (items 901–904) are automatically included along with those developed by the composition staff. While these global questions are more appropriate for making broad comparisons when evaluations are used for personnel decisions, rather than for providing instructors with specific information about what their students think of a particular composition class, their presence adds an institutional legitimacy to the survey which has proved useful when composition instructors have been nominated for university teaching awards.

Instructors are free to choose from among the items on the list, selecting those which they feel best reflect the goals of the specific course they are teaching. The instructions which accompany the list point out that the majority of the items are appropriate for most writing courses, while others, in particular items 14 through 19, are especially appropriate for courses which focus on academic writing. First-year teaching assistants and their mentors discuss the selection of items during a mentor meeting, thus connecting this evaluation with teacher preparation. In addition, most mentors meet individually with each teaching assistant in the group after the evaluations have been completed and summarized to discuss their implications. It has been particularly helpful to be able to meet with teaching assistants who have been discouraged by their evaluations, since frequently they pay more attention to their own ranking on the five-point scale than they do to the relationship between their own score and the mean score for all instructors who used that item. That is, they see their own "3" as an absolute indicator of their mediocrity, rather than as being higher or lower than the mean score. (It should be mentioned here that the computer form on which students complete the evaluation also has space on the reverse for additional comments. Teaching assistants receive both a printout that summarizes their ratings and gives the mean for each item and the original forms with the comments early in the semester following the evaluation.) New teaching assistants also need to be told certain facts of life about student evaluations, for example, that elective courses typically receive higher ratings than required courses like the one they are teaching, that professors receive higher ratings than TAs, and that there is a correlation between the grade a student expects and the rating (Braskamp, Brandenburg, and Ory 1984).

In the same way that the items on the preorientation survey and the mentor evaluation form are designed to help teachers consider specific aspects of their preparation, the items on the student evaluation form are intended to remind both the teaching assistants and the students who evaluate them about what constitute a good writing course and good pedagogy. Planning, revising, and editing writing are all included as positive activities, as are rhetorical concerns such as considering readers and purpose. More general items covering the instructor's availability to students outside of class and his or her promptness in returning papers also imply what our program expects of instructors.

Conclusion

Unfortunately and perhaps unavoidably, the concept of teacher evaluation connotes an appraisal which may lead to a personnel decision—to promote, to award a salary increase, to reappoint or not. While the preorientation survey obviously cannot be used for such purposes, it would be dishonest to claim that the mentor and instructor evaluation never are—or never could be—used to help make these decisions. Those people who are asked to serve as mentors are chosen because of their own knowledge of and interest and skill in teaching. While mentoring is undoubtedly hard work, it is also something of a prestige appointment, especially for graduate student mentors, and those who accept the positions have always fulfilled their responsibilities conscientiously and professionally. The instructor evaluation questionnaire does, however, play a role in some personnel decisions. Salary increases for teaching assistants beyond the across-the-board raises given by the graduate school are awarded on a merit system, and evaluations by students are one of several items considered by the committee which reviews merit. Also, in cases when mentors have indicated that a teaching assistant is not making adequate progress or when students have registered complaints, student evaluations may be considered along with other information in determining whether an instructor should be reappointed. Usually, however, in the infrequent cases in which there is a question about reappointing a particular teaching assistant, decisions are made on the basis of conversations with mentors, the instructor, students, academic advisors, and others directly involved with the particular situation. Thus, while these evaluations could be used to make personnel decisions, the need rarely arises for doing so. I would like to suggest that there are several reasons why this is so.

In the first place, as mentioned earlier, the items on the questionnaires have been selected with an eye to their consciousness-raising or informative power. When mentors know that people in their mentor groups will comment on the helpfulness of postobservation discussions, when teaching assistants know that their students will be asked to comment on whether they have learned how to use the library or document sources in a course on academic writing, they know that they should be having such discussions or should be teaching such strategies and skills. The very existence of the evaluations and the familiarity with them of those who are being evaluated may reduce the need to use the responses for personnel decisions.

In the second place, and more importantly, I believe, is the role all of these questionnaires play in creating an atmosphere of collaboration among teaching assistants, mentors, and writing program administrators. Even before they arrive, new teaching assistants are asked to contribute to their preparation by providing us with information about their interests and concerns. During their mentoring, they are asked to comment on how they are being helped and on what else they would like to learn. The fact that teaching assistants can suggest additional questions for the instructor evaluation and can choose from among a list of questions those which are most relevant to their goals in the course they teach increases the likelihood that these evaluations will be useful to them.

Ultimately, I believe, the participation of teaching assistants in their own preparation and evaluation serves to make our writing program more democratic and more centered on the success of the instructors. And by including them in a collaborative effort as people learning how to teach, we model for them ways of being teachers who include their students in collaborative, student-centered classes.

146

Works Cited

Braskamp, Larry A., Dale C. Brandenburg, and John C. Ory. 1984. *Evaluating Teaching Effectiveness: A Practical Guide.* Beverly Hills: Sage Publications.

Seldin, Peter. 1980. *Successful Faculty Evaluation Programs.* Crugers, NY: Coventry Press.

Weimer, Maryellen. 1990. *Improving College Teaching: Strategies for Developing Instructional Effectiveness.* San Francisco: Jossey-Bass.

Weiser, Irwin. 1990. "Surveying New Teaching Assistants: Who They Are, What They Know, and What They Want to Know." *WPA: Writing Program Administration* 14(1–2): 63–69.

12 Evaluating Teachers in Writing-Across-the-Curriculum Programs

John C. Bean
Seattle University

The proliferation of writing-across-the-curriculum (WAC) programs throughout the United States and Canada has complicated the already complex problem of evaluating teaching effectiveness. Traditional assessment instruments tend not to measure what WAC teachers do, and the pedagogical values that underlie the WAC movement are often disharmonious with conventional understanding of "good teaching." Moreover, many students resist the idea of writing in a non-English course. I recently received a telephone call from a distressed colleague seeking legal advice: A microbiology student at her institution had hired a lawyer to protest being graded on writing in upper-level science courses. While few teachers have been slapped with lawsuits for venturing into WAC territory, most have received their fair share of student evaluations peppered with student complaints about having to write.

The problem of evaluating WAC teachers is exacerbated politically by the blurry lines of authority in writing-across-the-curriculum programs. Who is doing the evaluating and why? A department chair for purposes of merit pay, promotion, and tenure? A WAC program director for purposes of program assessment or retention of teachers in "W" courses? Teachers themselves for the purposes of improving their teaching? More to the point, is being a good writing-across-the-curriculum teacher a plus or a minus within the university's real reward structure?

This last question, as I shall argue, is the crux of the matter. So long as using a write-to-learn pedagogy is seen as an aberration from standard teaching methods—as an "alternative" teaching style that students ought to encounter two or three times in their academic careers to tune up their language skills—then the assessment of WAC teachers will

Grateful acknowledgment is made to Fr. Stephen Sundborg, S.J., for permission to reproduce the assignment handout from his religious studies course; to Dr. Wes Lynch for permission to reproduce the extract from the introductory psychology course assignment; and to Dr. Kenneth Stikkers for permission to reproduce the group project philosophy class assignment.

remain a knotty but peripheral problem. WAC teaching will be rewarded as an "extra credit" activity in much the same way that we now
reward service. But it is my contention here that the pedagogical values
inherent in the WAC movement ought to transform an institution's
definition of good teaching throughout the curriculum. This is not to say
that all courses must be writing-intensive. It is to say, however, that all
courses ought to include *some* writing and that the pedagogy of many
courses across the curriculum ought to shift from a presentational or
"great lecturer" model of teaching to a dialogic, interactive model where
students use language to confront and explore problems, to make
meanings, and thereby to develop skills of inquiry, analysis, and argumentation. In attempting to support my thesis—which will no doubt
seem baffling to teachers and administrators unfamiliar with the writing-across-the-curriculum movement—I will begin by sketching out
what I see as the main traits of an excellent WAC teacher. Then, in section
two, I will try to show how current methods of teacher evaluation often
discourage rather than reward the pedagogical strategies of writing
across the curriculum. Finally, in the third and fourth sections, I will
suggest an approach to developing criteria for the evaluation of all
teachers—criteria in harmony with the theory and practice of WAC—
and suggest procedures for implementing these criteria using multiple
measures and peer reviews.

I

Establishing Criteria: The Traits of an Excellent WAC Teacher

To develop criteria for effective WAC teaching, one can begin by describing the traits of an excellent WAC teacher. These traits, however,
will vary according to the kind of WAC program in place at an institution. Institutions with clearly defined "W" courses may place higher
expectations on their WAC teachers than, say, institutions where WAC
programs are unstructured and voluntary. Since the definition of "WAC
teacher," as well as the criteria for excellence, necessarily varies from
institution to institution, I will attempt here only a generic description
of excellence. I should note that my description is based on a personal
conviction, which may not be universally shared, that being a WAC
teacher means more than just requiring writing in a course. To be a WAC
teacher, I believe, a teacher must also do the following: (1) integrate
writing assignments purposely into the course as a means of helping

students learn course content and develop the habits of inquiry and thought characteristic of the discipline; (2) use writing heuristically as a means of learning and thinking; and (3) improve their writing processes as a means toward improving final products.[1] Because the criteria for excellence must also vary according to the amount of institutional support provided for WAC programs, I will break this section into two parts. I will describe first what an excellent teacher might be like in an ideal WAC setting where class sizes and teaching loads are small enough to permit individual attention to students' writing. Second, I will describe how an excellent WAC teacher might adapt to less than ideal conditions such as large classes sizes, heavy teaching loads, or the demands of research or service.

Traits of an Excellent WAC Teacher under Ideal Conditions

Although there are many varieties of fine WAC teachers, they tend to share certain pedagogical values that give rise to common practices. On the basis of such shared values, evaluators can develop criteria for assessing WAC teachers.

First, an excellent WAC teacher has a working acquaintance with recent composition theory, especially the concept of writing as a process wherein the writer discovers, complicates, and clarifies ideas in the act of writing as opposed to merely transcribing already completed thought into correct language. As Peter Elbow (1973) puts it, "Meaning is not what you start out with but what you end up with. . . . Think of writing then not as a way to transmit a message but as a way to grow and cook a message" (14–15). This view of writing builds on the connection between writing and learning highlighted by James Britton and others who have studied the demands that writing places on higher-order reasoning (Britton et al. 1975; Fulwiler and Young 1982; Lunsford 1985; Maimon, Nodine, and O'Connor 1988). This heuristic view of writing encourages teachers to focus their writing assignments on the conceptual "stuff" of the course—the principles and theories, the data and information, the strategies of observation and thinking that constitute the subject matter of the course—and to use writing assignments that engage their students more deeply in this material. The teacher's role as grammarian and error-finder is diminished within this view of writing not because form and correctness are unimportant, but because they can't be separated from the larger concerns of the WAC teacher: how to teach inquiry, observation, analysis, and argumentation within the discourse conventions of the discipline.

Second, seeing writing as a way of learning and thinking, an excellent writing-across-the-curriculum teacher develops good writing assignments integrated with course content. Some of these assignments can ask for what James Britton (Britton et al. 1975) calls "expressive writing," that is, informal writing intended for the self rather than for audiences, writing for thinking out loud on paper, for raising questions, for seeking personal connections to new material (89–90, 140–46). For example, consider the following kinds of expressive writing tasks:

> You are Crito, and you have just listened to Socrates give his reasons for staying in prison and accepting execution. Given the value system you personally believe in, which of his reasons seems weakest to you and why? How does your value system differ from Socrates'? Why?
>
> I want each of you to flip a coin ten times and record the numbers of heads and tails that you get. Don't tell anyone your results. [Afterwards] Now freewrite your responses to these two questions: What do you predict will be the total number of heads obtained by all members of the class? How many people in the class do you predict will obtain exactly five heads and five tails? Explain your reasoning.
>
> Identify something that someone said in yesterday's class (either something the professor said or one of your classmates said) that particularly bothered you, confused you, or excited you. Explore your reactions to the comment by continuing the discussion on paper.

Expressive tasks such as these, whether assigned as brief in-class free-writes or as overnight journal entries, result in scrambled, thought-generating writing that can be rewarded for the potentiality of its ideas. Each values the student's personal voice. Each encourages students to see writing as a natural act, a familiar way of discovering and sharing ideas away from the teacher's red pen.

Teachers also need to give formal writing assignments calling for finished prose that goes through multiple drafts. An effective assignment is usually put in writing and distributed to students on a separate handout that describes the task itself as well as the intended audience, the assignment's purpose, its required structure and length, the process students are expected to follow, and the criteria to be used to evaluate the essay. Figure 1 shows an example of an effective assignment handout, one prepared by a religious studies professor at Seattle University.

A third trait of an excellent WAC teacher is effective course design. Because writing assignments must be integrated with course readings, lectures, and discussions, and because many teachers like to embed their assignments within a learning unit that incorporates journal

How paper relates to course goals:
There are three phases to this course: (1) Attending to experiences which evoke the "mystery of the self." Walker Percy's *Lost in the Cosmos* is used as a means for doing this. Thus, for the first part of the course, the most important thing is to raise questions around the human person as a mystery. (2) Looking to the religious experience of East and West in terms of how their experience has led them to respond to some of the questions about the mystery of the person raised in the first phases of the course. (3) In light of the above questions and responses, coming to a personal and conceptual synthesis of the religious or theological understanding of the human person. In each of these three phases you will be asked to write a paper which reflects the intent of the particular phase. This first paper focuses on Phase 1—raising questions about the mystery of the self.

Your task: Your task is to write an essay, based on Walker Percy's book as a model, that explores your own personal experience of the mystery of the self. Begin planning your essay by reexamining Percy's *Lost in the Cosmos*. This book is a goldmine of particular human experiences which point to the mystery of the self. . . . The *purpose* of your paper is similarly to raise the questions about *your* experience of the mystery of the person which you want to try to respond to in the rest of the course.

Structure: Organize your paper in a way similar to Percy's book. Therefore, in the first part of your paper, present experiences which for you evoke the mystery of the self. In the second part of your paper, try to present a hypothesis for the cause of the mystery which is evoked by your experience. In the third part of your paper, elaborate on the questions about the mystery of the self which you want to explore in the rest of the course from the perspective of religious experience.

Audience: Write your essay to your fellow classmates. Give your paper a "voice" that appeals to them.

Format: The paper should be three pages in length, a maximum of four. It should be typed and double spaced.

Criteria for Grading: My criteria for assessing your paper will be whether you follow the above structure, whether your paper shows reflection on your own experience, and whether an understanding of Percy is evident in how you write. Remember that this is a paper which raises questions; there are no wrong questions to raise. So do not be concerned about whether or not I agree with you.

Fig. 1. Example of an effective formal writing assignment.

writing, collaborative group work, and peer review, teachers must pay particular attention to the design of their courses. In doing course planning, the ideal WAC teacher would attend not only to what he or she will do in the classroom each day, but also to ways in which short write-to-learn activities might be assigned as homework to deepen students' attention to their out-of-class reading and studying. Thus, good WAC teaching demands considerable course planning.

Fourth, during the writing process itself, the excellent WAC teacher would act as coach, helping students learn the questioning and thinking skills needed to develop arguments within the discipline. Students' final written products can be substantially improved if the teacher intervenes effectively during the writing process. Teachers can choose among strategies such as the following: designing collaborative tasks for exploration of ideas, using peer reviews or teacher conferences to provide feedback on drafts, encouraging the use of writing centers, writing comments on rough drafts rather than final products, asking students to submit working thesis statements or argument abstracts well in advance of final due dates, allowing rewrites for better grades, and so forth. Coaching writing is especially time-consuming; teachers can be expected to perform this duty only when adequate institutional support is provided in terms of manageable class sizes and teaching loads.

Finally, the excellent WAC teacher is skilled at evaluating writing and providing feedback. When grading final products, teachers must turn from coaches to judges. They uphold standards of excellence within the discipline by grading rigorously. Also, by writing focused marginal and end comments on papers, they provide guidance for rewrites or for better strategies to use on succeeding papers.

Handling the Paper Load: The Excellent WAC Teacher under Less than Ideal Conditions

The preceding description of excellent WAC teachers applies mainly to those situations, such as in many "W" course programs, where content-area subject matter is to be taught in a writing-intensive way. Such courses require a substantial amount of writing and are often part of an institution's composition requirement for undergraduates. Much excellent WAC teaching, however, goes on outside of officially designated "writing-intensive" courses. A great number of WAC teachers want to use *some* writing in most, or even all, of their courses. They seek the benefits of a write-to-learn pedagogy without the concomitant exhaustion of a crushing paper load. It is essential that institutional reward structures recognize teachers for this effort. Simultaneously, it is essential that teachers find appropriate strategies for sustaining their WAC teaching without burnout. Often teachers can adapt to less than ideal conditions by continuing to give individual attention to students' writing but by cutting down the length or number of assigned formal papers. Also, they often develop innovative ways to assign nongraded expressive writing (in the form of journals, reflection pieces, marginal notes on readings, and so forth) that allow them to read some of their students' writing but not all of it. In this section I suggest several ways an excellent WAC teacher might assign writing even in large lecture classes.

Before suggesting such ways, however, I would like to digress momentarily to make a special plea to administrators for the welfare of WAC teachers. The great complaint of WAC teachers around the country is administrators' failure to appreciate the increased work load required by WAC teaching. Although there are ways to keep the increased work load manageable, WAC teaching of any kind involves taking on additional burdens. Administrators must eventually address this work load issue because failure to do so, as a study at De Pauw University makes clear, "will almost assuredly lead to a failure of a WAC program as a learning-to-write program" (Cornell and Klooster 1990, 10). The demands of WAC programs, Cornell and Klooster argue, are often in conflict with administrators' concerns for efficiency. If an institution tries to buy its WAC program on the cheap, it will eventually pay for it anyway through the hidden costs of faculty burnout. Thus, when I describe strategies for coping with less than ideal conditions, I do not intend to imply that institutions need not improve their support for WAC teachers.

With this caveat stated, I can suggest three ways that the excellent WAC teacher can use a write-to-learn pedagogy when faced with large class sizes or other serious constraints on time.

Nongraded, Expressive Writing

Perhaps the most common method in large lecture classes is to use short in-class freewrites to help students review previous material or to stimulate interest in what's coming. In-class freewriting gives students a chance to test their understanding of material and to ask questions. If the teacher collects the freewrites from a row or two of students each day, the freewrites give the teacher an opportunity to see students' thinking processes and to make teaching adjustments in response to their difficulties. Although ungraded in-class writing is a minimalist approach to WAC, it does emphasize writing as a mode of thinking and gives teachers in large lecture courses a way to maintain some contact with students.

"Microthemes" Graded Holistically with "Models Feedback"

A microtheme is a very short, one- or two-paragraph formal essay (sometimes submitted on 5 X 8 cards) in response to a problem set by the instructor (Bean, Drenk, and Lee 1982). Here is a typical micro-theme assignment from an introductory psychology course:

> In the morning when Professor Catlove opens a new can of cat food, his cats run into the kitchen purring and meowing and rubbing their backs against his legs. Explain to a student who has missed class this week what examples, if any, of classical conditioning, operant conditioning, and social learning are at work in this brief scene? Note that both the cats and the professor might be exhibiting conditioned behavior here.

For students to do well on assignments like these, they must first under-stand the course concepts. Microtheme assignments promote learning by stimulating out-of-class discussions and driving students toward more rigorous and extended thinking since concepts that initially seem clear get fuzzier as soon as the writer tries to explain them. Teachers can generally grade an individual microtheme in a minute or so if their only obligation is to attach a grade to it. (What makes grading papers time-consuming is writing out teacher commentary.) Rather than writing comments, teachers can provide feedback through in-class discussion of selected microthemes. Often students report that they learn more about writing from these discussions than from traditional comments on papers.

Group or Team Papers

Another approach, particularly common in business and technical fields, is a group or team paper. If 100 students work together in groups of five, the teacher needs to grade only twenty papers. In addition to reducing the paper load, team writing can help students develop skills in group interaction and interpersonal communication that will be invaluable in professional life. Figure 2 shows an example of a group paper assignment from a philosophy professor at Seattle University.

Summary: Criteria for Evaluating WAC Teachers

We can conclude this section by summarizing, in the form of a checklist of questions, the traits of an excellent WAC teacher as they might be used to guide development of evaluation criteria:

- Is the teacher familiar with major trends in composition theory and research, especially writing as a process and as a way of learning?

You will be assigned to a group to argue, using *empirical evidence*, for or against one of the following statements:

a. Capitalism provides fertile ground for the cultivation of virtue.

b. Equality, justice, and a respect for rights are characteristics of the American economic system.

c. A concern for ethics significantly undermines one's chances for success in a competitive market economy.

1. Consider material from Chapters 3 and 4 of your text as you begin to develop strategies for your argument. Also, be sure to define key terms in the proposition you are defending or refuting.

2. There will be no regular class Thursday, _____. You will have this time to use in whatever way your group judges best, e.g., brainstorming, strategizing, preliminary library research. Additional group meetings will have to be arranged by the groups themselves. Who will be responsible for what tasks and how the essay will be written are matters to be decided by the group.

3. Claims in the essays must be adequately and properly documented, e.g., footnotes or endnotes. Each essay must have a substantial bibliography— at least three good entries for each group member.

4. The instructor will evaluate each group essay, and everyone will evaluate the contribution of his/her group members to the group effort. Individual grades will be based upon both evaluations.

Fig. 2. Example of a group paper assignment.

- How effective are the teacher's assignments? Do they promote learning of course concepts and of thinking strategies used in the discipline? Are they effectively integrated into the design of the course? Does the teacher provide opportunities for active exploration of ideas through expressive writing, small-group work, or oral discussions?

- Does the teacher encourage writing as process? If conditions are favorable, does the teacher use effective strategies for intervening in the writing process (e.g., using peer-review groups, holding conferences, coordinating with a writing center, commenting on drafts, and so forth)?

- What standards does the teacher set for quality of final products? Does the teacher share grading criteria with students?

- Under less than favorable conditions, does the teacher manage to get some writing into the course by using nongraded writing, microthemes, group papers, or other strategies?

II

Deterrents to WAC: The Problem with Traditional Means of Evaluating Teaching

As the preceding discussion suggests, it should be possible for an institution to develop criteria for the assessment of WAC teachers. The problem, however, isn't how to develop criteria; rather, the problem is how to create an institutional environment in which these criteria are valued. In my experience, most institutions evaluate teaching by focusing primarily on the teacher's in-class performance as lecturer or discussion leader. The WAC movement, in contrast, places equal value on the kinds of out-of-class tasks assigned to students, on the teacher's acting as coach of thinking and writing, and on the teacher's use of written or oral activities to transform students from passive absorbers of knowledge into active critical thinkers.[2] Unfortunately, traditional methods of evaluating teaching often discourage the pedagogical strategies valued by WAC teachers.

A case in point is the widespread reliance on computerized student ratings, which, in my experience, can discourage teachers from requiring substantial writing. Although many students appreciate rigorous writing requirements in courses, others resent the unfamiliar burden of papers—like discovering "a cockroach in his soup" is how Richard Marius (1980, 8) describes the look one of his students gave him upon learning of writing assignments in a history course—and their dislike is apt to be reflected in their evaluations of the teacher. More than a few instructors have discovered that their reward for emphasizing writing in their courses has been a decline in their student evaluations at the end of the term.

The case of a young assistant professor at Montana State University, where I taught from 1979–1986, will illustrate the problem. His computerized ratings, which at MSU are sent to department heads for use in the evaluation of teaching, declined noticeably for the target courses in which he emphasized writing. (I have selected this teacher as an example because he was allegedly told by his department chair that his tenure case would be strengthened if he abandoned his emphasis on writing and went back to straight lecture teaching where he had earned high student evaluations.) His students' optional written comments for the writing-intensive courses, sent only to the instructor, clearly isolated the course features that students found unattractive:

Perhaps too much emphasis on writing.

We spent too much time on written assignments. The assignments were interesting but overemphasized. I would have rather covered more overall information and not concentrated so much on one problem. I must admit I learned writing techniques, but this was not a writing course.

Basically, the idea of trying to get students to put information they assimilate into their own words is a very good one. However, I was under the impression that this was a [name of discipline] class not a writing class.

I still feel that I didn't learn as much history of the period as I had hoped to; being a history major, I enjoy history, background, facts, etc., more than learning to write.

Of course, not all the discursive statements about writing were negative, but for this instructor, negative comments outweighed positive ones by two to one. Although many instructors are more successful than this teacher in their initial attempts to promote writing in their courses, students' potential hostility to writing nonetheless creates risks for teachers whose promotion, tenure, or merit pay depends at least partly on student evaluations.

Part of the problem, as teachers of writing-intensive courses often attest, is that a focus on writing in a content-area course tends to transform the view of knowledge implicit in the course's design. Whereas traditional courses tend toward a transmission theory of knowledge (I, the teacher, pass on concepts, theories, facts, and information to you, the students), writing across the curriculum tends toward a contextual, dialogic theory of knowledge in which students learn to join the discourse of the discipline (I, the teacher, want to help you learn how this discipline asks questions, forms hypotheses, uses reasons and evidence, and creates arguments). So when students object to writing in a content course, they are often objecting to the unsettling view of knowledge that the teacher is modeling. As the students quoted earlier make clear, what they want is a steady diet of information—set forth, they would probably say, in a series of scintillating lectures. What many writing-across-the-curriculum teachers value, however, is growth in students' ability to "talk the discipline"—to use the information of the course in meaning-making ways, in short, to inquire and to argue (Maimon 1979; Maimon, Nodine, O'Connor 1988; Bartholomae 1985; Bruffee 1984).

This transformation in the theory of knowledge has considerable implications for the way universities evaluate teachers. What those charged with teaching assessment must address, therefore, is the way that writing across the curriculum interrogates our definition of good teaching, an interrogation that may call not only for better measures than computerized student ratings, but also for different criteria.

III

Rethinking Criteria for Excellent Teaching:
Six Perspectives

Let's, therefore, change the direction of our questions by shifting point of view. Instead of asking how we can evaluate WAC teachers—a question that assumes that WAC teachers are an anomalous subset of teachers in general—let's ask how teachers in general ought to be evaluated in light of what writing across the curriculum adds to our understanding of excellent teaching. In short, what should be the major features of excellent teaching across the curriculum? While the specific criteria for excellence will vary from discipline to discipline and from setting to setting and must be decided locally by teachers and administrators at each institution, I suggest that these criteria be developed in light of six different perspectives.

   1. *Effectiveness in the classroom.* This perspective focuses on the teacher's conduct of class sessions. If the teacher primarily uses lecture, then traditional criteria for lecturing would apply—organization, timing, delivery, use of blackboard and overhead, enthusiasm, clarity, ability to respond to questions, and so forth. If a teacher uses alternative teaching methods, such as class discussion, Socratic questioning, or collaborative learning, then the criteria would vary accordingly (see Wiener 1986, for example, on strategies for evaluating collaborative learning). Traditional means of teacher evaluation, such as student evaluations and classroom visitations, are reasonably effective ways of assessing classroom excellence. This perspective—effectiveness in the classroom—seems the predominant one in traditional approaches to evaluating teaching.

   2. *Effective course design.* This perspective focuses on the entire learning environment created by the teacher—the out-of-class homework components of the course as well as in-class sessions; the integration of readings, assignments, and projects with classroom activities; the teacher's strategies for motivating learning, for demanding time on task, for teaching thinking and inquiry, and for testing; the relationship of the parts of the course to the whole; the articulation of course objectives; and the standards of achievement expected.

3. *Effectiveness at transmitting to students the conceptual and informational content of a course.* This perspective does not ask how well the teacher did in the classroom, but how well the student learned the course content—its ideas, theories, concepts, vocabulary, data, and information. In some disciplines—particularly in mathematics, the sciences, and related disciplines where courses are developmental and sequential—it is particularly important to measure teaching effectiveness at least partially by students' achievement at each level so that students are prepared for subsequent courses. In those disciplines where learning resists quantification—especially the humanities—measuring teacher effectiveness through student achievement may be notoriously difficult: witness the political and pedagogical debates over outcomes assessment. In such cases, however, indirect measures, such as course design and the development of challenging homework activities, help us see how the teacher attends to student learning. What makes this perspective particularly important is that we can't be certain there is a direct correlation between it and perspective 1. Do the most effective classroom teachers produce the most student learning? Economist Fritz Machlup (1979) has doubted this correlation on the basis of an experiment suggesting that students learn as much from bad teachers as from good ones (as determined by student evaluations and peer observations). Machlup studied the achievement of students from several parallel sections of an introductory economics course and discovered that students from teachers generally regarded as ineffective in the classroom scored as high on standardized tests as students from teachers considered excellent in the classroom. The highly rated classroom teachers, Machlup hypothesized, lulled students into believing that learning was easy. The incompetent classroom teachers, by leaving students confused or bored to tears, forced students to learn on their own through out-of-class study—and thus to learn as well or better. Of course, Machlup does not recommend that we become incompetent teachers but that we focus less on our own classroom performance and more on designing the kinds of complex reading and problem-solving assignments that challenge students to become independent learners. This perspective reminds us to distinguish between the teacher's classroom performance and the students' learning.

4. *Effectiveness at helping students enter the discourse of the discipline.* This perspective focuses on the teacher's ability to promote the habits of mind that characterize the discipline—teaching students how to question, hypothesize, gather and assess evidence, analyze, and argue within the discourse conventions of the discipline. In practice, evaluators using this perspective would focus on the teacher's design and

integration of problem-solving assignments that require students to use language to analyze and argue. They might also consider the quality of feedback the teacher provides on written or oral presentations, on the teacher's active use of office hours for conferences, and on the number and frequency of opportunities given students to use language actively for inquiry and argument.

5. *Effectiveness of relationships with students.* This perspective focuses on the professional/personal dimension of a teacher's interaction with students. It means generosity of time, keeping of office hours, helping students with questions, advising. The importance of this dimension varies greatly from institution to institution, with small liberal arts colleges perhaps placing the highest value on teacher/student interaction. At large research institutions, it is often graduate TAs who must provide this attention to individual students, but even then it is the supervising professor's job to ensure that such responsibilities are carried out in a caring way.

6. *Scholarly vitality.* Although often counted under the category of "publication and scholarship" rather than "teaching," scholarly vitality is a hallmark of a great teacher, one who models what it is like to be an inquiring, active member of a scholarly community. This perspective focuses on the intellectual rigor of a teacher's courses, on their being up-to-date, on their being infused with the teacher's own spirit of inquiry, on the teacher's serving as an active model of the learner, scholar, and writer. Teachers, for example, who can bring their own rough drafts into the classroom or who can explain to students the kinds of research problems they are currently posing for themselves are inviting their students into the conversations of their disciplines.

If colleges and universities used all of the preceding perspectives to develop criteria for evaluating teaching, then writing across the curriculum would not be seen as an optional pedagogical strategy that some professors "add on" to their courses. Rather, it would become an essential strategy for meeting the criteria. As teachers shift their focus from their own classroom performance (perspective 1) to the quality of student learning (perspective 3), the value of write-to-learn assignments that promote deeper engagement with course readings and more productive use of daily study time becomes obvious. Moreover, the effective use of writing assignments is perhaps the *only* strategy for initiating students fully into the discourse community of the discipline (perspective 4). It is through learning how to question and argue within a discipline that a student learns how the discipline investigates its unknowns and advances knowledge. It may be argued, of course, that it is possible to teach the discourse of a discipline without requiring writing. Through lectures, teachers can model the kinds of thinking and arguing that are practiced in the discipline, and through class discussions, laboratory projects, or computer simulations, teachers can engage students in the making of arguments. But no other linguistic activity requires the kind of sustained, disciplined thinking that writing requires. A good writing assignment keeps students on task in ways that in-class activities cannot match. Largely because writing is a recursive process of thinking and rethinking, of drafting and revising, it is the kind of homework requirement that most teaches students how the discipline makes meaning. Even teachers of mathematics and the most quantitative sciences are discovering the power of writing to enhance learning from courses as diverse as remedial algebra to advanced calculus and physics (Connolly and Vilardi 1989). Moreover, when teachers require writing, all the other perspectives come into play, also: The use of writing requires new attention to course design (perspective 2), provides new opportunities and challenges for interaction with students (perspective 5), and allows the teacher's own scholarly life to become a model for students (perspective 6). Finally, the use of writing often changes many of the teacher's traditional uses of class time (perspective 1).

My point, then, is that every teacher, to some degree, should be a writing-across-the-curriculum teacher. The use of writing is transformative: It transforms the view of knowledge in the classroom; it transforms students from passive to active learners; and it transforms the locus of "good teaching" from that of the teacher's classroom behavior to that of the whole environment in which learning occurs.

IV

Developing an Evaluation System
That Values a WAC Pedagogy

An important question yet remains. How can an institution develop a teaching evaluation system in which the above criteria are valued, that is, an evaluation system that sustains the vision of teaching and learning that characterizes the writing-across-the-curriculum movement? In this final section, I suggest some ways in which colleges and universities could develop such a system. The keys to a humane teaching evaluation system, I believe, are peer review and multiple measures. By "peer review" I mean two things: First, I mean that teachers are evaluated by a committee of peers—not peremptorily by a chair or dean or reductively by a computer that cranks out relative rankings on student evaluation scores. Second, I mean that the criteria for evaluation are developed communally by faculty, not imposed autocratically from above. The development of teaching criteria by faculty—often a year-long process if done in a truly collaborative way—is a wonderfully clarifying process for an institution and results in assessment criteria owned by those who will be assessed. Committees of peers, by consistently applying mutually developed and shared criteria, can make judgments derived from diverse and often nonquantifiable data. Through discussion and debate involving a wide range of data, committees of colleagues can arrive at decisions that are the best we can hope for in light of the conceptual and political complexity of the task. The question is, then, what information ought to be provided to peer-review committees? I suggest combinations of the following.

Student evaluations. Student evaluations, even if only one of the multiple measures, provide invaluable data to the peer-review committees. Whether collected as computerized scores or as raw narratives, they directly measure student satisfaction with a course and indirectly provide useful insights into a teacher's course design and effectiveness in the classroom. Also, when used comparatively against the scores from other teachers, they can give insights into a course's rigor.

To reward rather than penalize the use of writing-to-learn activities, institutions can add special assessment questions to traditional student evaluation forms. To minimize students' subjectivity, these questions can be stated as behaviors, with the response boxes indicating degrees of frequency (never, seldom, sometimes, often, frequently) or amount (none, a little, some, quite a few, a lot).[3] For example, institutions wishing to encourage more teachers to include writing in their courses could add the following statement for student response on their evaluation instruments:

> The teacher included evaluated out-of-class writing assignments as part of the course requirements.

For institutions with writing-intensive programs, additional statements such as the following might be added to evaluation instruments to get student response:

> The teacher was willing to help students at the rough draft stage of writing or to allow students to rewrite papers.

> The writing activities for this course helped me learn concepts or thinking strategies in this discipline.

> Writing assignments and grading criteria were clear.

Once specific items concerning writing assignments become included on student evaluation instruments, the evaluation system itself will provide an incentive for teachers to require writing, whereas the widely used subjective formats, where students' dislike of writing can negatively affect a teacher's overall rating, often seem a deterrent.

Syllabi, copies of writing assignments, and other homework. In addition to student evaluations, teachers should submit copies of their course syllabi as well as copies of their writing assignment handouts, other homework given to students, and descriptions of in-class, active-learning projects. These data allow peer-review committees to assess a teacher's course design, its clarity and rigor, and its demands upon students. In determining the quality of writing assignments, review committees need to consider factors beyond just the presence of writing assignments or the amount of writing required. Not all writing assignments are good assignments, as we know from the thousands of dreary, data-dumping, quasi-plagiarized "term papers" churned out by students around the country. The crucial question is not whether the teacher requires writing, but whether the teacher requires writing in an effective, purposeful way. Are the writing assignments focused and clear? Do they engage students in constructive problem-solving activities? Are they integrated with other course activities so that they increase student learning and teach questioning, analyzing, and arguing skills? By reviewing writing assignments in conjunction with course syllabi and other homework, review committees can gain insights into a course's design, its scholarly vitality, and its attention to student learning.

Classroom observation. In order to supplement student evaluations, many institutions require classroom observations as another measure of a teacher's classroom effectiveness. In a write-to-learn classroom, however, teachers often use a variety of classroom strategies. Thus, in addition to observing a "lecture day" or "class discussion day," peers should occasionally observe a day when a writing assignment is being passed out or when the class is working in small groups. As Harvey Wiener (1986) has shown, the criteria for effective collaborative learning activities differ extensively from the criteria for effective lectures so that classroom observers must understand how different teaching strategies make different uses both of class time and of teachers' behind-the-scenes preparation time.

Teacher's self-evaluation. A teacher's self-evaluation allows the teacher to describe teaching pedagogy, to highlight the data he or she finds most important, to explain anomalies in the data, and so forth. If peer-review committees ask for a portion of the self-evaluation to address how the teacher integrated writing assignments into the course, these passages become important means of assessing the teacher's commitment to writing and the teacher's understanding of writing as a process of questioning, clarifying, and arguing. Or, if an institution prefers not to focus directly on writing, instructions for self-evaluations can ask teachers to address how they try to enable students as active learners and how they help them practice the strategies of inquiry, analysis, and argumentation within the discipline.

Conclusion

The writing-across-the-curriculum movement shifts the definition of good teaching away from the "great lecturer" model toward an interactive, problem-centered model wherein teachers create learning environments that inspire and challenge students toward active learning, thinking, and problem solving. The writing-across-the-curriculum movement—by emphasizing many dimensions of teaching—gives us an opportunity to rethink how we conduct teacher evaluations. By encouraging an evaluation system focused on the whole environment of teaching and learning rather than primarily on the teacher's classroom behavior, the writing-across-the-curriculum movement can help transform not simply the evaluation of good teaching, but its very definition.

Notes

1. Mahala (1991) distinguishes between the "expressivist" school of writing across the curriculum and the "formal" school. The goal of the expressivists is to enable students to use their own language—their own voice, style, language of nurture—to explore new concepts across the disciplines. The goal of the formalists, in contrast, is to teach students the new, strange discourse of each discipline. Mahala prefers the expressivist school because of its implicit attack on academic convention through its alignment with the revolutionary British language-across-the-curriculum movement of which it is the pedagogical heir. Given my own tendency toward consensual politics, I do not see these schools as radically opposed. For the purposes of this article, excellent WAC teachers can embrace either expressivist or formalist goals. For a view similar to my own, see McLeod (1987). McLeod uses the terms "cognitive" versus "rhetorical" rather than "expressive" versus "formalist," but the distinctions drawn by her and by Mahala are essentially the same.

2. George Hillocks (1986) of the University of Chicago contrasts the "teacher-centered" or "presentational" mode of instruction (classroom lectures or teacher-led class discussions) with what he calls the "environmental mode" of instruction, in which the teacher designs a series of integrated problem-solving tasks that require students to work in groups to create arguments. Hillocks' investi-

gation suggests that the environmental mode is significantly more effective than teacher-centered modes at increasing students' ability to use course concepts in written arguments. Although his research focuses on instruction in writing classes, his findings can be readily extrapolated to other disciplines. His findings suggest that a problem-centered mode of instruction—the kind valued in much WAC teaching—produces the greatest student progress.

3. For a description of student evaluation instruments based on teacher behaviors rather than on students' subjective evaluations, see W. W. Ronan (1972).

Works Cited

Bartholomae, David. 1985. "Inventing the University." In *When a Writer Can't Write: Studies in Writer's Block and Other Composing-Process Problems*, edited by Mike Rose, 134–65. New York: Guilford.

Bean, John C., Dean Drenk, and F. D. Lee. 1982. "Microtheme Strategies for Developing Cognitive Skills." In *Teaching Writing in All Disciplines*, edited by C. Williams Griffin, 27–38. San Francisco: Jossey-Bass.

Britton, James, Tony Burgess, Nancy Martin, Alex McLeod, and Harold Rosen. 1975. *The Development of Writing Abilities (11–18)*. London: Macmillan Education.

Bruffee, Kenneth. 1984. "Collaborative Learning and the 'Conversation of Mankind.'" *College English* 46: 635–52.

Connolly, Paul, and Teresa Vilardi, eds. 1989. *Writing to Learn Mathematics and Science*. New York: Teachers College Press.

Cornell, Cynthia, and David J. Klooster. 1990. "Writing Across the Curriculum: Transforming the Academy?" *WPA: Writing Program Administration* 14(1–2): 7–16.

Elbow, Peter. 1973. *Writing without Teachers*. New York: Oxford University Press.

Fulwiler, Toby, and Art Young, eds. 1982. *Language Connections: Writing and Reading across the Curriculum*. Urbana: National Council of Teachers of English.

Hillocks, George. 1986. *Research on Written Composition: New Directions for Teaching*. Urbana: Educational Resources Information Center/National Council of Teachers of English and National Conference on Research in English.

Lunsford, Andrea. 1985. "Cognitive Studies and Teaching Writing." In *Perspectives on Research and Scholarship in Composition*, edited by Ben W. McClelland and Timothy R. Donovan, 145–61. New York: Modern Language Association of America.

Machlup, Fritz. 1979. "Poor Learning from Good Teachers." *Academe* 65: 376–80.

Mahala, Daniel. 1991. "Writing Utopias: Writing Across the Curriculum and the Promise of Reform." *College English* 53: 773–89.

Maimon, Elaine P. 1979. "Talking to Strangers." *College Composition and Communication* 30: 364–69.

———, Barbara F. Nodine, and Finbarr W. O'Connor, eds. 1988. *Thinking, Reasoning, and Writing*. New York: Longman.

Marius, Richard. 1980. "Faculty Indifference to Writing: A Pessimistic View." *WPA: Writing Program Administration* 4(2): 7–11.

McLeod, Susan H. 1987. "Defining Writing Across the Curriculum." *WPA: Writing Program Administration* 11(1–2): 19–24.

Ronan, W. W. 1972. *Evaluating College Classroom Teaching Effectiveness.* PREP Report no. 34. Department of Health, Education, and Welfare No. 72-9.

Wiener, Harvey S. 1986. "Collaborative Learning in the Classroom: A Guide to Evaluation." *College English* 48: 52–61.

13 Evaluating Teachers in Computerized Classrooms

Deborah H. Holdstein
Governors State University

> Collier's error in this vision as well as his error in research is that he sees only the technology. (Pufahl 1984, 93)

So pronounced John Pufahl in 1984, in vehement response to a study by Richard Collier (1983) in which Collier "didn't see significant improvement in the quality of students' writing" after sitting them before computers in his composition class (Holdstein 1987, 53). Although Collier's major point is most useful for my emphasis in the following essay, it is inadvertently so; as Pufahl notes, "Collier neither took part in the computer-writing process nor pointed out to the students where they might need to revise" (53).

Why would a brief debate that occurred in the early 1980s merit attention today? Despite conference programs that would seem to indicate the prevalence of research and practice regarding the possibilities of hypertext and the virtual reality environment, many English departments and writing programs still struggle with the basics of integrating technology into their writing curricula. Even within the mosaic of areas known as composition studies, it is likely that those doing the evaluating will have had little or no introduction to the theory and practice of technology's appropriate uses in the classroom. This difficulty multiplies when one considers that most English department chairpersons specialize in areas other than composition, and it further compounds for those composition specialists in the humanities, the social sciences, or other cross-disciplinary divisions in which the chair might come from a field well removed even from English studies. (Mine, for instance, specializes in criminal justice.)

And therein lies the rub—or perhaps just one of many—when a composition instructor chooses to use the computer as part of the writing curriculum. On the one hand, the introduction of technology can encourage a fresh look at writing program goals, at lines of reporting

167

and responsibilities. Departments and writing programs must first reiterate and possibly rearticulate the goals and strategies of the writing program itself; make clear its lines of reporting (Does the composition specialist serving as director of writing have the final word on the evaluation of teachers in the program?); and reinforce an administrative atmosphere that rewards quality instruction (particularly since many innovative faculty who use technology, take the considerable time to do so, and write about their work are untenured and might be taking time away from more traditional forms of research). Within the context of a particular department, technology seems to complicate an already complicated and often controversial process of evaluation for writing instructors.

Do we "see" the instructor's emphasis on the technology when we evaluate? Do we look solely at the way in which the instructor fosters the writing process? Do we evaluate the actual processes and procedures of the instructor using the computerized classroom or just those tangible outcomes—hard-copy drafts, overall student success? How might evaluating an instructor who uses an electronic classroom—whether the instructor uses it in part or its entirety—complicate other, relatively new types of teaching strategies that themselves defy traditional forms of evaluation: the collaborative classroom, for instance, and peer-revision groups? The evaluation of teachers who use technology must be seen in the larger context of the program itself. Yet the evaluator must pay attention not only to issues of program philosophy and of pedagogy, and to the role of the computer in teaching and learning, but also, importantly, to reaffirming the individual, that is, affirming the value of varying styles of teaching writing-as-process and recognizing the myriad possibilities for excellence among disparate, but effective, ways of teaching.

Evaluating teachers of composition on their use of computers is an essential component in determining the overall credibility of any composition program, and in my view, it must be part of a process that begins even *before* the instructor enters the electronic classroom—in fact, it is neither possible nor desirable to separate evaluation from training (and hence its intermingling throughout this essay). Any reliable director of composition worth her salt will certainly train graduate students and other new instructors before they are permitted to teach; she will interview carefully and observe the teaching of those who come with experience to determine the philosophical underpinnings of their pedagogy. To allow anyone with computer experience to implement it in the classroom, or worse yet, to mandate that it be done without any provision for training within the context of that particular institution, would be as irresponsible and potentially threatening to students' literacy as handing a grammar workbook (of all things) to a new instructor and saying, "Go to it." Simply put, inappropriate use of or emphasis on the computer might actually *impede* the writing process, reinforce misapprehensions about writing-as-process (indeed, reinforcing writing-as-product), and even more dangerous, give students the misguided sense that they are somehow less responsible for the quality of their writing after word processing than before. As with any form of evaluation, how can we possibly evaluate fairly that which we haven't beforehand delineated with care?

Directors of composition or chairpersons might feel somewhat remiss to have learned of technologically based writing impediments after the fact. As with any other mode that enhances writing instruction, or any method of writing instruction itself, the instructor's particular assumptions, understanding of the impact technology might have on her or his students, and philosophical perspective on the teaching of writing itself are essential; we as administrators cannot wait until the fifteen-week semester is over to ascertain whether technology has or has not been used in concert with the philosophy of the composition program.

In the discussion that follows, I will examine a handful of issues, ones that might be considered when evaluating an instructor who uses the computer within the writing curriculum. I will assume only rudimentary knowledge of technologically supported classrooms on the part of the readers—since it appears that those are the people who, more often than not, are doing the evaluating—building further on the concerns I have raised regarding the use of technology within English departments and composition programs.

Educating the Instructor, Educating the Student: Don't Forget the Basics

Using the computer to help students find their individual writing processes changes the writing classroom, but it does not change this important fact: the computer is an *enhancement* tool—it does not, in and of itself, improve the writing process. And here the Collier/Pufahl example becomes particularly relevant: simply put, if one's beginning students do not understand, beforehand, the process of revising their writing, then they will not know how to revise it before the looming presence of a computer screen.

Consequently, a certain type of education becomes extremely important for both the teacher and the student—what I call "philosophical immersion"—well before the computerized writing class begins.

Why? Most importantly, to disabuse both the teacher—and then, in turn, the student—of misguided assumptions about what the computer might or might not do to enhance the writing process; to ensure that instructors teach writing-as-process, teach it well, and understand recent composition theory; to ensure that instructors have attempted peer-revision processes or other collaborative methods of writing instruction in nonelectronic classrooms, effective methods that lend themselves naturally to electronic environments; to help instructors learn to use technology flexibly, i.e., that choosing to use the computer is not necessarily an all-or-nothing proposition; and perhaps even most important, to educate talented writing instructors, before they enter the computerized classroom, about the choices they will have to make—no longer "Which word processing software?" as much as "Will I/When will I permit my students to use style checkers or spelling checkers?"

A *good instructor of writing* who uses the computer (note my emphasis) can be evaluated as precisely that—an instructor of writing. However, certain other evaluation parameters must first be developed in teacher-training sessions or through informal discussion with the composition supervisor. For example, along with effective teaching of writing-as-process, does the instructor emphasize the limitations as well as the strengths of the computer? Such advice might take the following form for students, clearly demonstrating the writing-centered philosophy of the instructor. (This information—in various formats, depending on the course and audience—actually appears as an addendum to my syllabus.)

- A draft is not necessarily good simply because it looks good when it comes out of the printer.

- Working at a computer does not absolve the writer of responsibility for careful proofreading, revision, editing; if anything, it increases that responsibility.

- When one writes at the computer, the instructor does not become less important, nor can the computer take the place of the teacher. Rather, the computer reconfigures the instructor's essential role as expert, guide, and interactive agent in helping students as they learn to write more effectively.

- There is no single best method for using the computer to accomplish one's writing needs. As writers become more familiar with the computer and relevant software packages, they find that they prefer certain procedures that vary according to individual tastes and styles. Often, familiarity with technology and the writer's freedom in using it can depend on appropriate guidance and recommendations from composition instructors as the writer acquires confidence *as* a writer—and then as a "computer-writer," using the computer to whatever extent she or he desires in combination with so-called "traditional technology"—pen and paper, for instance (Holdstein 1987).

Experienced, confident teachers are the most appropriate and effective choices to be first in line for the computerized classroom; ironically enough, however, it is often the novice, the new teaching assistant, who is most eager to take on the challenges of technology and who is most amenable to trying something new in the classroom. Consequently, there are caveats for both seasoned and novice teachers alike, warnings worth considering going into as well as during the evaluation process. The instructor experienced in process-based composition theory and practice will need different training from the novice, but he or she may not have as much computer experience as the newly minted graduate student. However, the new instructor will not have the substantive teaching experience of his or her counterpart. Hence, this new instructor will be less able to respond quickly in an informed, spontaneous way to opportunities or concerns in the electronic classroom, situations, especially in front of the screen, which require the instructor to immediately draw upon substantive, process-based composition pedagogy.

The chair and director of composition need to pose additional questions before the computer-writing effort begins, the "flip side" of which might then serve for the evaluation process. Several of these raise important issues that might form the basis for colloquia concerning the use of computers in the curriculum, a useful forum during which experienced and less experienced instructors share an ongoing process of exchange about computers, student writers, the composing process, and (often too significant, unfortunately) the practical banalities (banal practicalities?) of computer use that affect not only access to computers, but also teaching and learning. The following is a select grab-bag of concerns listed in no particular order or emphasis, a list that might surprise some given its fairly basic contents. (I have learned through my visits to other campuses that I can never assume anything, even among those who have already implemented technology in their classrooms.) To merely *initiate* the necessary conversation among teachers, and between teachers and the writing supervisor, I'll elaborate on several of the items in the list:

- What is the program's or instructor's position on the students' use of style checkers? Spelling checkers? How will students be trained in their appropriate use? When? What is an inappropriate use? Why might one's attitude about this deceptively simple point reflect other philosophical positions about technology that might impede writing-as-process?

- Will there be an effort toward a "paperless classroom"? Is such an effort desirable? Why or why not? How would traditional methods of evaluation apply?

- What if there are not enough computers for the number of students in the composition course? What does the instructor do?

- Will the instructor have to demonstrate the use of a variety of types of software as part of the teaching strategy? If not, is the instructor not using the computer effectively? What if there's "nothing good" on the market?

- Computer-writing classrooms seem really noisy. What will the evaluator think? What about control in the classroom?

- How well must the instructor know the software in order to use it?

- Will the instructor have to use the computer classroom for every session? If not, where will the instructor be evaluated? Must the instructor be a computer expert? A computer-writer?

- How will the department need to reconfigure tenure criteria to encompass computer-related teaching activities?

- What if the instructor is not in the lab with her students during every class period? Is this a waste of resources? How will the chair or composition director evaluate this situation? What other people in authority will have an impact on these concerns, with agendas other than the most effective ways to teach writing? How will evaluators respond?

The Spelling Checker/The Style Checker

One might well wonder why I've put this on the list—at the head, no less. The extent to which students feel responsible for their own writing—empowered, in fact, to improve, to change for the better no matter what their level—can be modified to a greater or lesser extent by the ways in which instructors encourage this empowerment. Uninformed use of spelling checkers or style-checking software can sometimes lead students—particularly writing-anxious, beginning ones—to believe that they can depend significantly on the computer to do things for them, things, in fact, that writers should determine for themselves. If students all too often confuse editing with revision, the computer will only deepen that confusion unless the students first become confident revisers/editors. After all, a spell-check run-through won't assist the student in finding out which *it's* to use; whether or not she wants to use *there* or *their* or *they're;* whether or not it's *affect* or *effect;* potentially reinforcing confusion about errors of spelling versus errors of meaning. More significantly, however, misguided use of the spell checker reinforces the unfortunate notion that surface correction—that the paper "looks good"—is sufficient.

In fact, one of my colleagues learned this lesson all too well. An artist and an experienced writer, he attempted to spell the word that describes the figure used in department store windows to model clothing. On his own, he had written "mannekin," and when the spelling checker passed over it without comment, he assumed that it was an alternate to the correct spelling—"mannequin." Had he not checked the dictionary, the results might have been embarrassing: evidently "mannekin" is a rarely used term for "little man."

The same holds true with style checkers, yet their most appropriate use, in my view, might also indicate to student writers the fallibility of computer software that purports to judge writing—that the "bottom line" is the student's own judgment regarding any particular piece of work. David Dobrin (1990) has written a series of essays regarding the misguided information perpetrated on writers by style checkers. But one example of wildly inappropriate use might be the following: an instructor was asked how her basic writers could be encouraged to check sentence-level errors after they had drafted essays and worked to revise those drafts. Her response? "Oh, *Grammatik* will check that *for* them!" Egad! Not only is style-checking software often inaccurate, but to allow students to depend on it as if it were an example of what I always call "biblical inerrancy"—particularly when students haven't yet learned what they need to work on at the sentence level—does not in the least serve our students' literacy. At best, style checkers are suggestions waiting to be considered and (for me, the happiest scenario) suggestions more often than not successfully refuted by the writer herself. The software should be used to underscore the writer's empowerment and responsibilities, to reemphasize the computer's limitations; too many instructors allow students to take style checkers as gospel, and, left without guidance, student writers all too readily follow the program's "advice" as if they were plugging numbers into *Turbo Tax* (a tax-preparation program that "figures everything out" for the user) and seeking the "bottom line."

What does all this mean for teacher evaluation? Misguided use of software products can, indeed, impede the writing process—perhaps inadvertently teaching students exactly the opposite of what the otherwise well-meaning, process-based instructor intends. Depending on the evaluation process of an institution's particular composition program, the *means to the end* in the computer classroom might be considered as carefully as the student writers' overall success—just as we consider "process" and not merely "product" in writing.

The Paperless Classroom? Types of Software? Rethinking the "Appropriate" Classroom for Writing

Nowhere is it written that composing at the computer dictates a paperless environment. While several of my colleagues elsewhere have used this technique with varying degrees of success, I wonder, overall, about the point and its efficacy for most writing programs. Why bother? The computer-and-paper-and-ink environment best supports process when the instructional techniques reinforce it: for instance, the student composes part of an essay at the computer, produces hard copy, brings it to a peer-revision group, marks it up with pen or pencil after considering her own revisions and the comments of others, and then returns to the terminal to revise, perhaps to do more writing and/ or composing at the computer. Thus, methods old and new flexibly interact and, in my experience, best emphasize writing-as-process by allowing for individual styles of composing. But then, how might we evaluate teachers using such methods?

Just as with "traditional classrooms"—in this case, nonelectric classrooms—in which instructors rearrange chairs and students frequently meet in peer-composing/peer-revision groups, the computerized environment offers new challenges for evaluation. It has been said that instructors using newer collaborative techniques often receive lower evaluations from observers than teachers whose authority seems more obvious through their positions at the head of the class, near the blackboard; the computer-writing teacher might also suffer the same fate unless the evaluator is aware of these issues. A good, productive classroom can be noisy, busy, with people looking over other people's shoulders, brainstorming, talking, debating, asking for help, offering help. A savvy director of composition will already know this instructor well and will be able to tell immediately if the instructor has "flexible control"—that is, if the students are doing exactly what they are supposed to be doing, even if, on first impression, the classroom seems otherwise, indeed, seems rough-and-tumble.

Should computer-writing teachers be evaluated on the basis of how many different types of software products they use? No, but the ways in which they use the software, including word-processing packages, might be considered. For instance, drill-and-practice software—software that is, in effect, the electric version of a multiple-choice examination—seems all but useless in the teaching of writing. I'd shudder to find that any instructor in a classroom or even in a tutoring session in a writing center would think it profitable to place a student before a drill-and-practice program on, say, subject-verb agreement and then assume that this learning by rote is adequate or even desirable.

However, in my own classroom, I've used older drill-and-practice programs when I am able to follow up immediately with writing-as-process. For instance, when there are only ten computers and my class bears fifteen, I'll have students work on drafts at the computer while others revise their drafts or compose further at nearby tables. When a student has reviewed subject-verb agreement with a drill-and-practice or tutorial program, we work immediately to ensure that the "lesson" becomes part of the actual composing process. In fact, the limitations of the software and having fewer computers than necessary have worked to important advantage for writing-as-process: we emphasize stages in the composing process, of working collaboratively, of finding one's own composing process. And most importantly, class size, of necessity, becomes limited by virtue of there being relatively few computers for the number of students in the class.

Evaluators must keep in mind that an instructor who uses only word—processing software isn't necessarily short-changing the students; indeed, "only" word-processing software is most desirable, and I usually discourage colleagues from using other software products, having instructors create, instead, their own activity files. Evaluators might want to consider whether the instructor has indeed encouraged students to use word-processing software creatively, for instance, creating files with the students to help them brainstorm or revise.

However, much of this evaluative process will depend on the extent to which the computer is implemented, and here there are few right or wrong percentages or answers. Some instructors merely introduce students to composing at the terminal, encouraging them to do their computer writing outside of class but not emphasizing it for in-class work; some instructors do this because of preference, others because of institutional limitations on computer use for their classes. Indeed, many of the formats for using the computer in the writing classroom depend to a great extent on institutional contexts: the availability of the computer lab, whether classes can be brought to the lab (as opposed to a "drop-in only" lab), whether classes meet in the lab during every session or whether students do most of their computer writing outside of the class session and then work mostly with hard copy in class, and so on. Other instructors have the opportunity to meet every session in the lab;

I have always preferred to divide our time between the lab and the so-called "traditional classroom" for discussion and group work.

Department chairs and writing program directors will have to keep these variables in mind, too, as they evaluate: If something "didn't work," how much of it had to do with the instructor's best efforts, or, more likely, a failure on the part of support services in the laboratory? If the chair passes by the department lab (if the department is so fortunate) and Professor X's 10 a.m. class isn't there, the chair might then assume that the students are in their other classroom doing something quite productive; establishing a lab does not necessarily indicate that it will be in use every minute of the day (although it might). Remember, there is no one preferred model for using the computer to teach writing, nor is there one preferred format. Computer-writing classrooms should allow for individual styles of teaching and learning, just as any good traditional classroom would. But the point is this: even if every computer in the lab falls apart, even if the 10 a.m. class has had its disks erased, even if the 10 a.m. class arrives to find that the members of the 10 a.m. management class thought *they* had the lab that day, is the instructor making certain that *the students are still writing, learning to be confident, skilled writers, no matter what?*

What the Evaluators Can Do

As with any new approach to teaching—or in fact with actual movements in teaching, such as writing across the disciplines—those empowered to evaluate must create a climate that appreciates, that values, good teaching in the writing program, computerized or not. I mentioned earlier that such innovative methods involving collaboration often meet with less-than-favorable reviews at evaluation time; since use of the computer can often tax even the most flexible viewpoints within traditional English programs, most important, then, is the chair's creating a favorable climate in which teachers choosing potentially innovative methods for teaching writing can be evaluated fairly. Would it be fair to allow Professor X, who is somewhat hostile to the use of computers to begin with but a pillar of the department, to evaluate Professor Y's computer-writing class? Obviously, the evaluator must be someone not only open to the possibility that appropriate use of the computer might enhance the learning process, but also someone familiar with the issues I've raised in this essay.

In a fashion similar to methods in writing-across-the-disciplines programs, instructors using computers to enhance the writing process might also be evaluated on the activities assigned to students both in and out of class (particularly if the class meets in the computer lab every time) and on the ways in which the teacher becomes a facilitator of student writing (as opposed to being a traditional lecturer). But again, these nontraditional ways of teaching must first be valued by the department in other contexts in order for them to be valued when manifest in the computer lab; effective leadership on the part of the chair and writing director are therefore primary.

Consequently, those who will evaluate must first evaluate themselves—their own facility with computer writing, their own knowledge of the issues surrounding computer use in the teaching and learning of writing, and their own perspectives on nontraditional teaching methods. Moreover, evaluators must focus on the same criteria they would use in so-called traditional classrooms: course design; strategies for motivating student learning; complex, problem-solving assignments. For instance, how does the instructor in the computer lab attend to the "at-onceness" (Berthoff's term) or the "recursiveness" of the writing process on the part of her students? How do the syllabi and class assignments define the rigor of the writing class enhanced by computers?

Given my inherent distrust of many evaluation policies while acknowledging their inevitability, I also suggest that chairs and WPAs resist creating specific, formulaic criteria for evaluating computer use in the curriculum; to do so might undercut individual styles of teaching, to require a lockstep pattern in an area that defies quantification. Most essential, then, is training before the computer-writing effort; the chair can assist by helping the instructor make sure that appropriate forms of support (lab time, technical assistance) are available and in place. The chair might also want to work out a system whereby the instructor/writing specialist team-teaches the word-processing software with the help of a lab assistant, preferably before the semester begins. (Such a plan helps to alleviate the concern that the instructor won't be teaching writing at first, but advanced secretarial skills. We still cannot assume that all of our students come to us having had access to computers, or, specifically, to word processing.) To leave training entirely to a lab assistant with little or no interest in writing can be a serious mistake: it is impossible to teach word-processing software without there being any writing to it, so his or her judgment (regarding style or spelling checkers, for instance) shouldn't be the first encountered by a student writer.

After this litany of "most importants," however, I reiterate yet another: most important is an administrative atmosphere in which quality instruction is valued (both traditional and innovative, with differing ways to use class time that can be equally valuable); in which instructors are well trained; and in which faculty are trusted when things don't always seem traditionally "predictable"—and in which students, not the teacher, seem to be at the head of the class. Indeed, technology can provide the opportunity to re-vision a department's program, providing a spotlight that can be both flattering and harsh and one which highlights weaknesses as well as strengths. For instance, has the department generally tended to devalue collaborative work? Technological enterprise will only exacerbate the problem.

Evaluating computer use in the writing curriculum depends on many variables, with several factors often beyond the instructor's control. But appropriate use of the computer—not how much or how often it is used—is the benchmark of evaluation along with the all-important "bottom line": the students' having been challenged by a process-based curriculum that has enhanced their writing abilities with or without technology, the computer perhaps having played a role in that process.

What we *don't want* is a Collier/Pufahl redux: the parent who recently remarked to me, "Oh, yes, my daughter took a writing class with computers last fall at _____ State. And she learned so much about *computers!*" Like other innovative movements or techniques within composition studies, effective use of the computer can move us away from the paradigm of the solitary scholar to interactive, student-centered learning, away from a presentational to an environmental form of learning (George Hillocks's term); but the effective teacher of writing with the computer must first and foremost be an effective teacher of writing and its processes.

Works Cited

Collier, Richard. 1983. "The Word Processor and Revision Strategies." *College Composition and Communication* 34: 149–55.

Dobrin, David. 1990. "A Limitation on the Use of Computers in Composition." In Holdstein and Selfe, 40–57.

Holdstein, Deborah H. 1987. *On Composition and Computers*. New York: Modern Language Association of America.

———. In press. "I Sing the Body Electric: The Near-Literary Art of the Technological Deal." In Myers.

———, and Cynthia L. Selfe. 1990. *Computers and Writing: Theory, Research, Practice*. New York: Modern Language Association of America.

Myers, Linda. 1993. *Computer Writing Laboratories*. Buffalo, NY: SUNY Press.

Pufahl, John. 1984. "Response to Richard Collier: 'The Word Processor and Revision Strategies'." *College Composition and Communication* 35: 91–93.

Index

Editor

Christine A. Hult is professor and assistant department head in the English department at Utah State University in Logan, Utah. She currently serves as the editor of the journal *WPA: Writing Program Administration* (the journal of the Council of Writing Program Administrators). Her research interests include computers in writing and program and teacher assessment, as reflected in recent publications in *Computers and Composition* and the *Journal of Advanced Composition,* as well as her textbooks *A Writer's Introduction to Word Processing* (with Jeanette Harris) and *Researching and Writing Across the Curriculum,* (2nd ed.). She is active in professional organizations, including WPA, CCCC, and NCTE.

Contributors

Mark A. Baker is currently an English teacher and concurrent enrollment instructor at Logan High School. He also serves as adjunct professor at Utah State University. He has taught at the high school level for ten years. He has also served as associate director of writing—supervising the composition program both on and off campus—at Utah State University. While in that position he helped to develop both the freshman composition and sophomore research-writing curricula at USU. He has published over forty of his essays in a variety of popular magazines.

John C. Bean is professor of English at Seattle University, where he directs the writing program. Active in the writing-across-the-curriculum movement since 1977, he has conducted numerous faculty workshops at colleges and universities across the United States and Canada. He is co-author of the textbooks *Form and Surprise in Composition: Writing and Thinking Across the Curriculum* (Macmillan, 1986) and *Writing Arguments* (2nd ed., Macmillan, 1991). He has also authored numerous articles on writing across the curriculum and on Renaissance literature. A former member of the executive board of the Conference on College Composition and Communication, he is currently a consultant/evaluator for the Council of Writing Program Administrators.

David Bleich works at the University of Rochester, supervising graduate students in their undergraduate teaching experiences, and teaching graduate and undergraduate courses in writing, literary response, rhetoric and style, women's studies, and Jewish studies. His most recent book is *The Double Perspective: Language, Literacy, and Social Relations* (Oxford University Press, 1988; paper, NCTE, 1993). Forthcoming from SUNY Press in 1993 is *Writing With: New Directions in Collaborative Teaching, Learning, and Research*, edited with Sally Reagan and Tom Fox.

Peter Elbow is professor of English at the University of Massachusetts at Amherst. Previously he has been a member of the faculties of SUNY at Stony Brook, Wesleyan University, Evergreen State College, the Massachusetts Institute of Technology, and others. His books include *Writing without Teachers; Writing with Power: Techniques for Mastering the Writing Process; Embracing Contraries: Explorations in Learning and Teaching; A Community of Writers* and *Sharing and Responding* (both with Pat Belanoff); and *What is English?*

Anne Marie Flanagan teaches at the University of the Arts and is completing her Ph.D. in English at Temple University. She has presented her work on classroom observations at various conferences and continues to research and write about the politics of evaluation.

Deborah H. Holdstein directs the writing program and coordinates English studies at Governors State University, located just south of Chicago. In addition to her essays on composition and the use of technology in composition studies, she has written on literary theory and the classroom, and issues concerning feminism and institutional politics. Her books include *On Composition and Computers* (MLA, 1987) and *Computers and Writing* (MLA, 1990), the latter co-edited with Cynthia Selfe. She is currently working on an anthology of literature for composition. Holdstein regularly presents at CCCC and MLA, and presents lectures to a variety of local and national organizations and workshops.

Jesse Jones serves as the executive director of the North Texas Community and Junior College Consortium at the University of North Texas. He has taught English in both the community college and university and is co-author of *Composition and Literature: Exploring Human Experience*. His administrative experience includes service as an assistant dean of academic affairs at the university and as writing program coordinator, division chair, vice president, and acting president at the community college. He currently serves on the editorial board of *WPA: Writing Program Administration* and as president of the National Council of Instructional Administrators, an affiliate council of the American Association of Community Colleges.

Joyce A. Kinkead is professor of English and associate dean of the College of Humanities, Arts, and Social Sciences at Utah State University, where she also directed the writing program for eight years. She is the former editor of *The Writing Center Journal* and the co-editor of *Writing Centers in Context* (NCTE, 1993) and *Houghton Mifflin English, 9–12*. She reviews for *College Composition and Communication*, *The Writing Center Journal*, and the *Journal of Advanced Composition*, as well as serving on the NCTE Editorial Board.

David E. Schwalm is associate professor of English at Arizona State University, where he served as director of composition from 1986–92. He is now associate provost for academic programs at Arizona State University West. Before coming to Arizona State, he was WPA at the University of Texas at El Paso, where he also founded the West Texas Writing Project. He has written articles on the rhetoric of biography and on various topics relating to rhetoric, composition, and writing program administration. He also makes regular presentations at CCCC conventions and WPA conferences.

Ellen Strenski is assistant director for Upper Division and Graduate Writing in the UCLA Writing Programs. In addition to co-authoring *The Research Paper Workbook* (3rd ed., Longman, 1991), *Making Connections Across the Curriculum: Readings for Analysis* (Bedford Books, 1986), and *A Guide to Writing Sociology Papers* (3rd ed., St. Martin's, 1994), she has published in many pedagogical journals on the subject of writing in diverse disciplines.

Michael J. Vivion is professor of English at the University of Missouri at Kansas City, where he directed the composition program and founded the Greater Kansas City Writing Project. Vivion serves on the editorial board of *WPA: Writing Program Administration* and is a referee for *College English* and *Research in the Teaching of English.* In addition to his journal articles and textbooks, he co-edited, with James Berlin, *Cultural Studies in the English Classroom* (1993). He also makes regular presentations at the NCTE annual convention, CCCC, and MLA. He demonstrates his commitment to improved teaching through his work as a consultant to educational institutions in the United States, Europe, and Africa. He is also an elected member of the Kansas City, Missouri School Board.

Irwin Weiser is associate professor of English and the director of composition at Purdue University. He is co-author of *Language and Writing: Applications of Linguistics to Rhetoric and Composition* and author of an introductory rhetoric, *Writing: An Introduction,* and has published in *WPA: Writing Program Administration, Composition Studies,* and the *Journal of Teaching Writing.* He currently serves on the editorial board of *WPA* and the *Journal of Basic Writing* and is a consulting reader for *College Composition and Communication.*

Edward M. White is professor and former chair of the English department at California State University at San Bernardino and former coordinator of the Upper-Division University Writing Program. Statewide, he has been coordinator of the CSU Writing Skills Improvement Program, and for over a decade was director of the English Equivalency Examination Program. His *Teaching and Assessing Writing* (1985) has been called "required reading" for the profession; he is now preparing a revised and expanded edition. In addition, he is the author of many articles on literature and the teaching of writing; he has written three English composition textbooks and has one more under contract. He is a frequent speaker at conferences and a consultant to various educational institutions in the area of writing and evaluation. He has twice been elected to the executive committee of CCCC. His most recent books are *Developing Successful College Writing Programs* (Jossey-Bass, 1989); *Assigning, Responding, Evaluating: A Writing Teacher's Guide* (St. Martin's, 1992); and (with Lynn Z. Bloom) *Inquiry: A Cross-Curricular Reader* (Prentice-Hall, 1993).